"All professionals want the same thing—a solid backlog of interesting and profitable clients—but few understand how to achieve it. *Book Yourself Solid* fills this gap with the most comprehensive and actionable toolkit that you'll ever need for building lifelong clients."

> **—Andrew Sobel, author of *Clients for Life*
> and *Making Rain***

"I believe that Michael Port has written the definitive book on marketing your professional services. Not only is every page full of immediately useful tips and tactics to attract clients and build your business, but *Book Yourself Solid* also is fun, easy to read, and incredibly inspiring."

> **—Mitch Meyerson, author of *Success Secrets of the Online
> Marketing Superstars***

"You can't afford not to buy this book! *Book Yourself Solid* gives you a proven system for generating business on your own terms, and you'll fall in love with yourself by the time you're done reading it! This book is a keeper because Michael Port is a keeper—he's sincere, engaging, funny, and brilliant. Struggle is strictly overrated, so pick up a copy of this must-read today."

> **—Kim George, author of *Coaching into Greatness:
> 4 Steps to Success in Business and Life***

"Launch–Accelerate–Prosper! *Book Yourself Solid* really is a turnkey success system for solo practitioners and entrepreneurs to attract as many clients as they desire. It's amazing."

> **—David Perry, Managing Partner of Perry-Martel
> International and coauthor of *Guerrilla Marketing
> for Job Hunters***

Additional Praise for *Book Yourself Solid*
(From People Just Like You)

"By using just the strategies taught in the first couple of chapters, I got booked solid in just two weeks! I'm still getting a huge flood of new clients, and now I only take on the projects that I want to work on, and I even have a waiting list of clients who have already sent in their contracts! I can't wait to see what the rest of the book will bring!"

—Graphic Designer—Erin L. Ferree,
elf design, www.Elf-Design.com

"It only takes a few minutes to realize Michael's sincere desire to help you get more clients. His passion is contagious. Marketing and acquiring new clients was overwhelming. We were going in many different directions with little success. Thank goodness *Book Yourself Solid* was easy to follow and implement. In just six weeks our business had a 300 percent increase in clients. What we learned in the first chapter was worth a hundred times the price of the book. In fact, *Book Yourself Solid* is priceless."

—Health Club Owners—Christine and Kevin King,
Get Fit!, Inc., www.LifeOnlyBetter.com

"Michael Port's *Book Yourself Solid* will answer your prayers. Not only will you be booked solid in short order but you will also have a waiting list of your perfect clients begging to get a taste of you! 'How?' you ask. You'll have to read the book, but let me say that Michael has helped me create laser-like focus and clarity in my business that has ignited prosperity in every corner of my life. I'm unstoppable! Follow his magical blueprint outlined in the pages of *Book Yourself Solid*, and you'll be unstoppable, too. Michael, I cannot thank you enough for breathing new (superhuman) life into me and my business."

—Wedding Consultant—Tshombé Brown,
www.YourSignatureWedding.com

"*Book Yourself Solid* is the most amazing and complete business building and marketing system I have seen. I used to struggle in my practice, and more money was pouring out than was coming in. In desperation I took class after class with well-known gurus in business building, but I didn't see any results. But because of *Book Yourself Solid*, I now have new clients signing up for my services every day, and they are the high quality clients I love to work with. Thanks to Michael and his astonishing system, I have a waiting list of clients who want to work with me. Michael's system is the only one I feel 100 percent confident to recommend. If you only buy one book this decade, buy *Book Yourself Solid*."

—Career Advisor—Liselotte Molander, CEO of LKM Communications, coaching and training group of companies, www.LiselotteMolander.com

"What an inspiring and motivating marketing system you have created! From the first page of *Book Yourself Solid* until the last, I received invaluable tips and techniques to grow my business and myself. By using your thought-provoking exercises, I was booked solid by Chapter 7! I credit my business growth to the carefully crafted sequence in the system where you urged me to release those clients who did not fit the profile of my ideal client so that I could clear the way for those who do. I learned the value of thinking even bigger about my purpose and my passion and found the courage to respond with increased enthusiasm and planning. Thank you, thank you, thank you!"

—Freelance Writer—Ann Leach, www.AnnLeach.net, Co-Author, *Goal Sisters: Live the Life You Want with a Little Help from Your Friends*

"Quite simply the best book on how to attract and secure clients that I've ever read. *Book Yourself Solid* helped me increase the number of clients that I serve by more than 50 percent and skyrocketed my revenues by over 60 percent. It's a fantastic, inclusive, and extremely useful book. Frankly, it may be the last book I ever read on marketing and selling my services."

—Acupuncturist—Mike Berkley, L.Ac., Doctor of Acupuncture (RI), Director, The Berkley Center for Reproductive Wellness and Women's Health, www.BerkleyCenter.com

"Michael Port's *Book Yourself Solid* is only one of a rare handful that I can recommend without reservation. It deserves extraordinary praise. Michael is clearly an expert in his chosen field, and he has the wonderful ability to present his material with passion and heart. He is extraordinarily committed to providing astonishing value and delivers the material in ways that make it educational, doable, practical, and fun. Any reader who applies him- or herself will make tremendous and guaranteed progress to becoming booked solid. Many thanks, Michael, for your fantastic contribution to my business expansion."

—Spiritual Teacher—Ron Wypkema, Founder and Director, The Clarity Institute, www.NowTeachings.com and www.theNowSolution.com

"Michael Port has done it! He encapsulated into one book all the answers and information I've been searching for. As a financial planner I am completely responsible for filling my practice, and *Book Yourself Solid* reveals every possible strategy I need to fill my practice with all the clients I want. The best thing about *Book Yourself Solid* is how easy and exciting it is, not only to read but to actually follow through on the direct and clear action steps that Michael gives you. I've seen my practice go from sometimes sort-of-booked to oh-my-gosh-this-is-amazing booked solid! In fact, I got what Michael said I would—a relentless demand for my services. Thank you, Michael."

—Financial Planning Specialist—Michael D. Thompson, Smith Barney, A Division of Citigroup Global Markets Inc., www.fc.smithbarney.com/michaelthompson

"Michael, you are an amazing gift. I have to thank you for the *Book Yourself Solid* system. Before you, I was lucky to sign up a client per month. I'd struggle my way through training program after training program, but since *Book Yourself Solid*, my confidence is through the roof and I am passionate about how OnAirPublicity.com is helping authors and others become great radio guests. I'm happy to say that in the last two weeks I've booked four new clients and my inbox is flooded with leads. I am now booked solid, and it's only going to get better. You showed me how to believe again. I can't thank you enough!"

—Public Relations Consultant—Wayne Kelly, On Air Publicity, www.OnAirPublicity.com

"How do I get more clients? The nagging question gnawed at me constantly—until *Book Yourself Solid* appeared. I had read so many books, enrolled in so many courses (most of them awful), listened to tapes and CDs, all of which promised miracles. There were no miracles. I was struggling and didn't want to buy into yet another empty promise. Then a recommendation for *Book Yourself Solid* from a trusted colleague came, and my business has never been the same. Admittedly, I have not completed all of the exercises in the book because—guess what? I got booked solid so fast! Anyone wanting more clients *has* to learn from Michael how to take the necessary actions to get booked solid. Many claim to have the secrets to marketing, but Michael's claim is that he will teach you how to create relentless demand for your services, and he does!"

—Business Management Consultant—Lorraine Lane,
www.LaneBusinessConsulting.com

"The one word that sums up Michael Port for me is *empowering*. These days, there is a 'business coach' on every street corner, hawking their 'proven path to millions.' They perpetuate the idea that those of us who are in the process of growing successful businesses don't really know what we need to know, that we can't trust our own insights and must rely on theirs. Michael is exactly the opposite. Yes, he does share strategies to book a business solid, and they are great strategies. Yes, he does share insights from his own experiences, and they are really useful. But at every turn, in every page, he reminded me that I do in fact know what I need to know and that I can trust my own insights. That, for me, is what made *Book Yourself Solid* so powerful—it put the controls in my own hands and cheered me on to win."

—Marketing Firm Owner—Trish Lambert,
4-R Marketing LLC, www.4RMarketing.com

"*Book Yourself Solid* is absolutely fantastic. It takes you from kinda-sorta knowing what you want to do to oh-my-gosh taking your dreams and business to the next level. With concrete exercises and carefully outlined lessons, you will be booking yourself solid in no time."

—Blogging Expert—Andy Wibbels, Author, *Blogwild!*
***A Guide for Small Businesses*, www.AndyWibbels.com**

"When I was first exposed to *Book Yourself Solid*, I was desperate. I had left my six-figure corporate position to pursue my dream of being an entrepreneur, but it was feeling more like a nightmare. Even before finishing *Book Yourself Solid*, I'm delighted to say that not only am I just two clients from being booked solid, I've matched my previous monthly income and I've also landed corporate consulting opportunities that I would never have expected until year two of being in my practice. *Book Yourself Solid* will transform your business and your life!"

—Executive Coach and Consultant—Pat E. Perkins,
PMP, CPCC, www.ExodusCoaching.com

"I can finally talk about what I do without getting tongue-tied! I spent months (okay, years) fumbling with different ways to describe my business and getting polite nods in return. Even in print, it took paragraphs to explain with any sort of clarity. Now I have a succinct, dynamic way to tell people what my business is all about and why it should matter to them. And that has done wonders for my self-confidence and assuredness in reaching out to potential alliance partners (another lesson from *Book Yourself Solid*). If you want to get booked solid and experience the freedom that comes with clarity and you are ready to finally focus your energies, then read *Book Yourself Solid*."

—Online Business Owner—Terri Zwierzynski,
Solo-Entrepreneur.com, Inc., www.Solo-E.com

"As a CPA, I have always found marketing difficult, something I didn't really like doing or want to do and consequently didn't do. Of course, I have known for some time that I *needed* to market my practice. But I really had no idea how to go about it until I began *Book Yourself Solid*. And I have been really surprised at how this system has given me such a different outlook about marketing. There is *so* much more to marketing than I previously envisioned. Now instead of dreading and avoiding marketing, I am excited about it. And I am beginning to see much *bigger* possibilities than I did before. Michael, you have provided such a wealth of information that is so valuable and so practical, so essential and so helpful. One of the most important, significant, and meaningful benefits I have received from *Book Yourself Solid* is a new awareness that I really want to make a difference in people's lives, that I want to do more than just technically excellent tax work, and that our work is meant to be a reflection of who we are and not just a paycheck."

**—Certified Public Accountant—Thomas L. Codington,
Asheville, North Carolina**

"Michael Port is a genius. He has taken away every excuse for not growing our business with practical, step-by-step strategies and refreshing perspectives on marketing one's business or practice. Grab the book, a note pad, and a pen because the ideas you capture will transform the way you play the game."

**—Certified Speaking Professional—Mark Rosenberger,
CSP, Author, *SPLAT!*, www.NoSplatZone.com**

"Would I recommend *Book Yourself Solid* to other people? Heck, yeah! I never thought I'd be the kind of person who would go on and on about something like this, but I've been recommending it to everyone who I think needs it because I've gotten so much out of it (and continue to get so much out of it). I am truly grateful for *Book Yourself Solid* and for Michael. Thank you so much. You've helped me make my business reflect more of me in a way that is accessible to others and that excites and inspires me when I think about it, talk about it, and do the work of making it grow to amazingly booked-solid proportions."

**—Celebrity Life Coach—Rebecca Soulette,
www.RebeccaSoulette.com**

"I have read dozens of marketing books and consider myself a pretty good marketer, so it's hard for me to find a book that would impress me. But I think that *Book Yourself Solid* is so innovative and unique in its approach that I absolutely consider it to be in the same category as Seth Godin's *Unleashing the Ideavirus*. It made me feel great about marketing my business. Those business owners who feel guilt or shame about their marketing absolutely need this book! Very mind-shifting!"

**—Professional Association Founder—Milana Leshinsky,
Association of Coaching and Consulting
Professionals on the Web, www.accpow.com**

"Reading *Book Yourself Solid* is fun and exhilarating. Michael's enthusiasm is contagious, and the exercises in the book facilitate personal and business growth. Michael possesses an exceptional gift in his ability to perceive how people limit their growth. He helps people identify and break old patterns and gain new perspective about what prevents them from fulfilling their goals. Michael's talent lies in his insight and wit; he uses a combination of humor and charm to help people make important shifts in their thinking. Eloquent, playful, and direct, *Book Yourself Solid* is a gem."

**—Psychiatrist—Alexander Kolevzon, M.D., Author,
*Psychiatry Essentials: A Systematic Review***

"Thank you so much for *Book Yourself Solid*. I'm sure you hear this a lot from your readers (because it's so true), but I think you're really amazing. I haven't been inspired by a book in a very long time. It feels like you're working with me personally—and it helps! I feel more grounded, in control, and seasoned—and I'm completely booked solid. You have a very special place in my heart."

**—Yoga Teacher—Jodi B. Komitor, Founder, Next
Generation Yoga, www.NextGenerationYoga.com,
Co-Author of *Complete Idiot's Guide to Yoga
with Kids***

Book
Yourself
Solid

Book Yourself Solid

The Fastest, Easiest, and
Most Reliable System for
Getting More Clients Than
You Can Handle Even if You
Hate Marketing and Selling

Michael Port

WILEY

John Wiley & Sons, Inc.

Published by John Wiley & Sons, Inc., Hoboken, New Jersey.
Published simultaneously in Canada.

For general information on our other products and services please contact our Customer Care
Department within the United States at (800) 762-2974, outside the United States at (317) 572-3993
or fax (317) 572-4002.

Wiley also publishes its books in a variety of electronic formats. Some content that appears in print
may not be available in electronic books. For more information about Wiley products, visit our web
site at www.wiley.com.

Library of Congress Cataloging-in-Publication Data:

Port, Michael, 1970–
    Book yourself solid : the fastest, easiest, and most reliable system for
getting more clients than you can handle even if you hate marketing and
selling / Michael Port.
        p.   cm.
    Includes bibliographical references and index.
    ISBN 978-0-471-78393-0 (cloth)
    ISBN 978-0-470-28190-1 (paper)
    1. Selling.   2. Marketing.   3. Strategic planning.   I. Title.
HF5438.25.P67   2006
658.8—dc22

                                                          2005034029

Printed in the United States of America.

10 9 8 7 6 5 4 3 2 1

This book is a love story disguised as a business book,
a love story between you
and all the inspiring clients you will serve.

Contents

Acknowledgments

The first line of the acknowledgments section in virtually every book goes something like this: *To list everyone I want to thank for their contributions to this book would be a book in itself.* You really don't know how true that is until you write your own book. Few great things are accomplished by one person. The words that follow don't even begin to describe the magnitude of my gratitude for all of the people, not only those mentioned here, who have shaped this book and have made my life and work as spectacular as it is today.

To my team at Michael Port & Associates LLC . . . thank you: Lisa Wilder, for your immeasurable courage and extraordinary talent. I kiss the ground you walk on. This book is as much yours as it is mine. Raquel Morphy, for making it possible for me to be creative. You are my rock. Gayla DeHart, for teaching me more every day about what it means to truly serve our clients. I am blessed to work with you. Peggy "Done!" Murrah, for keeping us all sane. Kathy Green, for holding my hand selling this book in a matter of weeks. Ann Leach, for cutting the fat and taking this book from good to great. Bonnie Jean, for contributing your expertise. Howell Burnell, for your creative genius and your big heart. Verna Wilder, for your careful attention to the manuscript. Now I know where Lisa gets her talent. Matt Holt, my editor at Wiley, for your expertise. You have honored my vision with your collaborative spirt.

To my teachers . . . thank you: Dave Buck, for being there at the beginning. Hal Macomber, for being a beacon in a sea of mediocrity. George

Lyons, for your commitment and high expectations. Ken Risch and Ron Van Lieu, for teaching me to express myself. Tim Sanders, Dan Pink, Michael Gerber, and Seth Godin for serving as professional role models in absentia.

To my business partners . . . thank you: Mitch Meyerson, your music inspires me. Let's keep playing. Bea Fields, for being a true leader. Julie Hunt, for being one of my favorite partners of all time. Caitlin Adams, here's to the impending release of *The Think Big Manifesto*.

To my clients . . . thank you: I think I learn as much, if not more, from you than you do from me; my deepest thanks for giving me the opportunity to serve you. You inspire me every day.

To the members of The Think Big Revolution . . . thank you: for demanding that I show up in the world in the biggest way that I possibly can. I live for you.

To my family . . . thank you: Mom, Dad, it is because of you that I have the wildly outlandish belief that I can do anything. Pearl, for putting up with my oversized ego and teaching the next generation. Alex Kolevzon, Neal Kaufman, and Ben Terk, you will always be the harbor lights that guide me home. The Schaffers for putting a roof over our heads when we didn't have two nickels to rub together. Da Mama and Ken Egger and the rest of the Egger clan—you are pure love. Grandma Evelyn, for your unconditional love.

To my beautiful, talented, and spirited wife, Shannon . . . you most of all deserve my thanks. You make it possible for me to stand in the service of my destiny. I love you very much.

To my son Jake . . . the goodness in you is the fire that fuels me.

Foreword

Face it—you'd rather be doing your life's work than filling the sales funnel or getting the word out. Every day that you aren't on a project is like an airplane seat that goes unsold. You picked up this book because you know that you can do better and grow stronger in your business acumen.

You will get out of this book only what you put into it. Don't just skim the pages to pick up pointers. Take the time to do each exercise. Take a few weeks to move through this book. Pretend you are in school and striving to be at the top of your class. *Because you are.* When you look at your calendar next year and you aren't happy with all the white space, pick this book up and go through it again more slowly.

Readers are leaders, and I believe this is true with you. Read this book as a business owner and think about the suggestions as you build a culture for your company. Who knows how big your enterprise might get? You might be hatching the next Big Blue, and you will need a common set of values to guide your vision into the future.

I resonate with this book's technology and its spirit. Most of Michael's advice comes from a point of view that can be summed up in two statements:

- Make yourself emotionally attractive.
- Live on the right side of the Law of Reciprocity.

Emotionally attractive people win the popularity contests that make up your life. Yes, you have experience, work ethic, and talent. But you still lose the business and see it floating to a competitor, and you *know* you are better than that competitor. Why? The emotional brain is two dozen times more powerful than the logical brain. The customer wants a great experience, not just good consulting or an effective process. The attention you pay to the emotional experience of working with your customers may be the best way to differentiate yourself and build a contagious brand.

Book Yourself Solid outlines practical ways to improve your ability to produce positive emotions in other people—from·how you serve them to how you network with them. Above all, the book gives you advice on building a consistent process in your business. And process is very *likeable* to a customer.

The Law of Reciprocity must be respected to build a sustainable business of any kind. This law postulates that in almost every case people reciprocate, especially when it comes to energy or generosity. If your customers receive added value from you, they will add energy to your relationship. If you give them enough (either intangible or tangible), you will reach a tipping point where they become loyal to you and start to market you to their sphere of influence.

Conversely, when you create an I-win-you-lose scenario for the customer, your business is cyclical. You get a job, finish it, and return to selling yourself. You have to slug out every business win. This is true even when you are the excellent provider that behaves like the Soup Nazi on the *Seinfeld* TV show.

Either you build a business that obeys this law or you don't. There is probably no in-between. Greed is too powerful and faith is too fragile. This book will guide you into a set of practices that always give your customer a reason to give back and wish you the best.

As I finished reading this book, I was reminded of an old saying that should send you deep between the lines as you read it:

Long after people forget what you said or did, they will remember how you made them feel.

—Tim Sanders,
     author of *The Likeability Factor: How to Boost Your*
     L-Factor and Achieve Your Life's Dreams (Crown Publishing)

Author's Note

An unfulfilled vocation drains the color from a man's entire existence.
—Honoré de Balzac

In early 2000 I was utterly dissatisfied and completely disillusioned with my work as the vice president of programming at an entertainment company. The environment felt like a prison—long hours, unresponsive colleagues, and no personal engagement. Sound familiar? I decided to embark on a new career path as a professional business coach and consultant: *a service professional.* I secretly passed the time reading, researching, studying, and honing my coaching skills. After much planning, my *freedom* date was marked on every calendar in my apartment with a huge victorious smiley-face. My resignation letter was signed, sealed, and ready for delivery. I could hardly keep my legs from sprinting out the door to follow my heart and head (both of which had checked out long ago).

On that auspicious day, I received the envelope with my bonus inside, ran to the bank, cleared the check, and proudly delivered my letter of resignation. The joy, pride, and satisfaction that I felt at that moment was incredible. I floated home and woke up the next day to plunge into my career as a solo business owner serving others.

However, I didn't bask long in the glory before I realized I was in for trouble.

Call me crazy, but I really thought clients were just going to fall into my lap. I expected them to meet me, fall in love with me, and trade their money for my services. Instead, I moped about my very costly New York City apartment, panicking, feeling sorry for myself, and doing trivial busy work that wasn't going to generate a dime of income.

Within six months I was desperate, which heralded a new phase of my life. I was fed up. I'd reached my limit. I was not going to throw in the towel and give up on my career as a solo business owner. I visualized the next 10 years with my fiancée, Shannon, the love of my life. But to tell you the truth, I felt that Shannon was going to marry a complete failure. When we met I made six figures a year; now I made very little.

My innate need to support and provide, to serve the people I was meant to serve, kicked into high gear one cold New York morning. Rather than dwelling on the cold reality of my financial struggle and the bitter temperature outside, I worked every single day for no less than 16 hours to succeed and pay the bills. I poured myself into more resources and studied everything I could get my hands on about how to attract clients, communicate effectively, sell, market, and promote my services. First and foremost, I wanted to learn how to love marketing and selling by turning it into a meaningful spiritual pursuit.

It worked. Within 10 months I was booked solid with more clients than I could handle. But the personal checks I cashed were not the most valuable part of my business. It was the turnkey system I was building that propelled my business and income every month. I started sharing my success secrets with a small group of trusted clients, and I watched their success unfold before my eyes. I could hear confidence, pride, and accomplishment in their voices. Their businesses boomed!

My clients, who were service professionals of all kinds, started to get booked solid: massage therapists, mortgage brokers, accountants, therapists, acupuncturists, dentists, hair salon and spa owners, bookkeepers, web and graphic designers, business consultants, chiropractors, professional organizers, financial planners, virtual assistants, health care providers, insurance brokers, attorneys, personal trainers, travel agents, photographers, physiotherapists, Pilates and yoga instructors, coaches, realtors, reflexologists, sales professionals, naturopaths, and others were getting more clients than they could handle.

I immediately began to engineer a completely replicable system that I could pass on to you. That system is the Book Yourself Solid™ system, and you're holding it in your hands, the same system I've been teaching to thousands of other service professionals around the world in my live seminars and Book Yourself Solid Intensive Coaching Programs. The results are powerful.

Ninety-three percent of clients who have used the Book Yourself Solid system have increased the number of clients they serve by over 34 percent and increased their revenue by over 42 percent within the first year.

I'd like to impress upon you right now how realistic it is for you to become a successful self-employed professional. According to Daniel Pink (*Free Agent Nation*—citing a study by Anne E. Polvika, "Into Contingent and Alternative Employment: By Choice?," reported in the 1996 October issue of *Monthly Labor Review*), "Full-time independent contractors earn an average of 15 percent more than their employee counterparts." Daniel Pink also shows (from a study by Aquent Partners) that, "Independent professionals are twice as likely as W-2 workers to have personal incomes above $75,000 per year." In fact the Aquent Partners study shows that one in four Americans is now an independent professional.

That's great news, isn't it? It proves that you've made the right choice to go it on your own. But I'd like for us to think even bigger. What if you could do more? Just imagine how different your life would be if you were earning $10,000 each and every month. How about $20,000, $30,000, or $40,000 each month? *Amazingly* different! I can tell you from personal experience it opens up a world of possibilities. And you can do it too! Because the Book Yourself Solid system will get you up and out into the world in the biggest and most profitable way.

You need to learn the skills necessary to promote your work and become the go-to person in your field before it's too late. I don't want you to start working through this book two years from now. I want you to reap all of the rewards that you deserve now. If you haven't yet reached the level of success you expected or wanted in your business, there is only one small change you need to make. Put yourself smack-dab in the middle of my Book Yourself Solid system. This one move will get you sprinting (not running . . . not walking . . . but sprinting!) to monthly income and personal satisfaction that will change your business—and your life. Think of all the freedom, abundance, profitability, and joy you can create for yourself.

There is no question that the Book Yourself Solid system can change your business and your life. Of course, it's up to you whether you'll take advantage of it.

You love what you do. You're great at what you do. You stand in the service of others, and you are a remarkable human being for doing so—now it's time to get booked solid.

I will show you the way to a profitable, meaningful, and absolutely booked-solid business, overflowing with as many clients as your heart desires, clients who energize and inspire you, clients with whom you do your best work, clients who will pay you handsomely.

I hope you feel the same exhilaration in building your independent business as I do every day. I expect that the Book Yourself Solid system will not only inspire you but will keep you keenly focused on learning and re-learning, experimenting and honing all that is within you. I am certain the secret to your success isn't just in the work that we do together. It lies within you. *Book Yourself Solid* will help facilitate your greatness.

We are all on this path together, learning from one another. We are all seeking joy, love, success, and happiness. I urge you to continue to trust that you are making a huge difference in the lives of your clients, yourself, and society as a whole.

Here's to you—to focusing on getting as many clients as your heart desires. It is my wish that you come to the Book Yourself Solid system with an open heart and mind. Completely remove, or at least set aside, any preconceived ideas fluttering in your head. Let this powerful process be revealed to you step by step.

The Book Yourself Solid way is one of abundance, joy, and meaning. It's my deep honor to hold your hand and walk you down this path. I've had the pleasure and fortune to serve thousands of other professionals just like you who want to build a service business based on their gifts, talents, and skills. And just like them, you inspire and energize me because you have dedicated your work to serving others. I know your successful break-through is near and will continue to be sustained by your faith, inner strength, and confidence.

As any silly, serious, significant, strategic, personal, or professional questions come up, please give me a shout. I'm always delighted to hear from you. Fire off any and all questions to me and my team at questions@book yourselfsolid.com. If there is anything I can do to serve you, please just ask.

Now, let's get to booking you solid!

Think Big,

Michael Port
The guy to call when you're tired of thinking small

Preface

The Book Yourself Solid system is supported by both practical and spiritual principles.

From a practical perspective there may be two simple reasons why you don't serve as many clients as you'd like to today. You either don't know what to do to attract and secure more clients or you know what to do but you're not actually doing it. The Book Yourself Solid system is designed to help you solve both of these problems. I will give you all of the information you need to book even more clients than you can handle; I will give you the strategies, techniques, and tips. If you already know what to do but aren't doing it, I'll inspire you into action and help you stay accountable so you build the business of your dreams.

From a spiritual perspective I believe that if you have something to say, if you have a message to deliver, if there are people you want to serve, then there are people in this world that you are *meant* to serve. Not kinda, sorta, because they're in your target market . . . but *meant* to—that's the way the universe is set up if you're in the business of serving others. If you don't understand this now, you will when you read this book and follow the Book Yourself Solid way.

The system is organized into three modules: Your Foundation, Building Trust and Credibility, and the Book Yourself Solid 7 Core Self-Promotion Strategies.

We will begin by building a foundation for your service business that is unshakable. If you are truly serious about becoming a super-successful service professional, you must have a steadfast foundation on which to stand. You will then be ready to create and implement a strategy for building trust and credibility. You'll be considered a credible expert in your field and you'll start to earn the trust of the people you'd like to serve. Then, and only then, will you execute the seven core self-promotion strategies, thereby creating awareness for the valuable services you offer by using promotional strategies that are based on your talents, strategies that feel authentic and honest.

To help you design a service business overflowing with clients who inspire and energize you, this book includes Written Exercises and Booked Solid Action Steps that will support you in thinking bigger about your business. Step by step I walk you through the actions you need to complete on the path to serving as many clients as your heart desires.

As a reader of *Book Yourself Solid*, you will want to retain your responses to the written exercises for regular review. I have prepared a complimentary downloadable workbook that includes all of the Written Exercises and Booked Solid Action Steps contained in this book. Simply visit my web site and download the workbook so that you may begin today to take the necessary steps to get more clients than you can handle.

> Go to www.bookyourselfsolid.com/workbook.htm right now and download your free copy of the workbook so you've got it in your hands before you turn another page.

You also have access to hundreds of additional resources and opportunities at www.BookYourselfSolid.com, all designed to assist you on your business-building path.

Before we begin our journey, please take a moment now to register at www.bookyourselfsolid.com/workbook.htm and get immediate access to your free workbook and other valuable free resources, like the networking forums and the client referral exchange.

While you'll no doubt get great value just from reading this book, the true value—and your success—lies in your decision to take an active role and to participate fully by doing the exercises, taking the Booked Solid Action Steps I've outlined, and connecting with other service professionals at www.BookYourselfSolid.com. In doing so, you will begin an evolutionary journey of personal and business development that will empower you to achieve the success you know you're capable of.

If you follow the system, it *will* work for you. No skipping, jumping, or moving ahead—the Book Yourself Solid 7 Core Self-Promotion Strategies are effectively implemented only after Your Foundation and Credibility Building Strategies are in place. One of the main reasons that service professionals say they hate marketing and selling is that they're trying to market without a foundation and credibility-building strategy, which is like eating an egg before it's cooked—of course, you'll hate it. So no matter how compelled you are to skip ahead, I urge you to *please* follow the system and watch the process unfold.

So many talented and inspired service professionals like you run from marketing and sales because they have come to believe that marketing and selling is pushy and self-centered and borders on sleazy. This old-school paradigm is not the Book Yourself Solid way; it is the typical client-snagging mentality. And you must *never* fall into the typical client-snagging mentality. If you do, you'll operate in a mentality of scarcity and shame as opposed to one of abundance and integrity.

Ask yourself these questions:

- How can I be fully self-expressed in my work to create meaning for me and those whom I serve?
- How can I work only in the areas of my greatest strengths and talents so that I can shine?
- How many relationships with people of purpose did I make and deepen?

- How can I better listen to and serve my ideal clients?
- How can I wow people with substance?
- How can I overdeliver on my promises to my clients?
- How can I cooperate with other professionals to create more abundance?

If you keep asking yourself these questions, if you set a solid foundation for your business, build trust and credibility within your marketplace, and use the seven core self-promotion strategies, you'll be booked solid in no time.

Ready to get started? Let's do it!

Module
ONE

Your Foundation

To be booked solid requires that you have a solid foundation. That foundation begins like this:

- Choose your ideal clients so you work only with people who inspire and energize you.
- Understand why people buy what you are selling.
- Develop a personal brand so you're memorable and unique.
- Talk about what you do without sounding confusing or bland.

Over the course of Module One, I'll step you through the process of building your foundation so that you have a platform on which to stand, a perfectly engineered structure that will support all of your business development and marketing, and—dare I add—personal growth. That's because being in business for yourself, especially as someone who stands in the service of others, requires constant personal reflection and spiritual growth.

Building your foundation is a bit like putting a puzzle together. We're going to take it one piece at a time, and when we're done you'll have laid the foundation for booking yourself solid.

1

The Red Velvet Rope Policy

He who trims himself to suit everyone will soon whittle himself away.
—Raymond Hull

Imagine that a friend has invited you to accompany her to an invitation-only special event. You arrive and approach the door, surprised to find a red velvet rope stretched between two shiny brass poles. A nicely dressed man asks your name, checking his invitation list. Finding your name there, he flashes a wide grin and drops one end of the rope, allowing you to pass through and enter the party. You feel like a star.

Do you have your own red velvet rope policy that allows in only the most ideal clients, the ones who energize and inspire you? If you don't, you will shortly. Why? First, because when you work with clients you love, you'll truly enjoy the work you're doing; you'll love every minute of it. And when you love every minute of the work you do, you'll do your *best* work, which is essential to book yourself solid.

Second, because you *are* your clients; they are an expression and an extension of you. Do you remember when you were a teenager and your mother or father would give you a hard time about someone you were hanging out with? Your parents may have said that a particular kid reflected badly on you and was a bad influence. As a teen you may have thought how very unfair that was, but the truth is that you are the company you keep. It's imperative for this reason to choose your clients as carefully as you choose your friends.

The first step in building your foundation is to choose your ideal clients, the individuals or businesses with whom you do your best work, the people or environments that energize and inspire you. I'm going to help you identify specific characteristics of individuals or organizations that would make them absolutely ideal to work with. You will then develop a rigorous screening process to find more of them. I'm also going to help you prune your current client list of less than ideal clients.

When I began my business I would work with anyone who had a pulse and a checkbook. Then I read an article by the late Thomas Leonard, author of *The Portable Coach*. He suggested that we choose our clients. He said we should work only with clients who are ideal for us. And thank goodness I took his advice to heart. Now I live by what I call the red velvet rope policy of ideal clients. It increases my productivity and my happiness, it allows me to do my best work, and I have more clients and referrals than I can handle by myself. And so will you.

For maximum joy, prosperity, and abundance, think about the person you are when you are performing optimally, when you are with all the people who inspire and energize you. Now think about all of the frustration, tension, and anxiety you feel when you work with clients who are less than ideal—not so good, right?

Wouldn't it be great to spend every day working with clients who are ideal for you, clients whom you can hardly believe you get paid to work with? It is completely possible once you identify who you want to work with and determine with absolute certainty that you will settle for nothing less. Once you do that, it's just a matter of knowing which of your existing clients qualify and how to acquire more just like them.

Dump the Duds

Author and business guru Tom Peters takes us a step further. In *Reinventing Work: The Professional Service Firm 50*, he challenges us to dump our dud clients. "Dump my clients?!" you exclaim. I can just hear your many protestations and exclamations of shock. "I thought this was a book about getting clients, not dumping them!" you counter. But Peters is referring to the *dud* clients—not all of your clients, just the duds. It sounds harsh, but think about it. Your dud clients are those you dread interacting with, who drain the life out of you, bore you to tears, frustrate you, or worse, instill in you the desire to do them—or yourself—bodily harm, despite your loving nature.

I'm well aware of the many reasons you *think* you can't dump your dud clients, and I know this can seem really scary early on, but hang in there with me. Embrace the concept and trust that this is sound advice from a loving teacher and a necessary step on the path to booking yourself solid.

Why have clients, or anyone for that matter, in your life who zap your energy and leave you feeling empty? In the first year of being in business on my own, I cut 10 clients in one week. It wasn't easy. It required a major leap of faith, but the emotional and financial rewards were astonishing. Within three months I had replaced all 10 and added 6 more. Not only did I increase my revenue, I felt more peaceful and calm than I ever had before, and I enjoyed my clients and my work more.

When I asked myself the question, "Would I rather spend my days working with incredibly amazing, exciting, supercool, awesome people who are both clients and friends, or spend one more agonizing, excruciating minute working with barely tolerable clients who suck the life out me?" I had no choice. I knew the temporary financial loss would be worth the payoff.

1.1.1 Written Exercise: To begin to identify the types of clients you don't want, consider which characteristics or behaviors you refuse to tolerate. What turns you off or shuts you down? What kinds of people should *not* be getting past the red velvet rope that protects you and your business?

1.1.2 Written Exercise: Now take a good, hard look at your current clients. Be absolutely honest with yourself. Who among your current clients fits the profile you've just created of people who should *not* have gotten past the red velvet rope that protects you and your business?

1.1.3 Booked Solid Action Step: Dump the dud clients you've just listed in the above exercise. It may be just one client, or you may need another two pages to write them all down. (Did I warn you that I'd push you to step out of your comfort zone? If I didn't, then I am now.) Is your heart pounding? Is your stomach churning at just the thought? Have you broken out in a cold sweat? Or are you jumping up and down with excitement now that you've been given permission to dump your duds? Maybe you're experiencing both sensations at the same time; that's totally normal.

Taking a Booked Solid Action Step is a bold action and requires courage. And courage is not about being fearless—it's about owning your fear and using it to move you forward, to give you strength. There is no more rewarding feeling than the pride you'll feel once you've moved past the fear to do what you set out to do. Maybe you'll find it easier to take it one step at a time. Start by referring out just one of those dud clients. The feeling of empowerment you'll have once you've done it will motivate you to continue pruning your list of clients until the duds have all been removed.

If you're struggling with the idea of pruning your client list, keep in mind that it's for your client's benefit as much as it is for yours. If you're feeling empty and drained, or frustrated and dreading the interaction with the client, you're giving that client far less than your best, and it's both of you who are suffering for it. You owe it to these clients to refer them to someone who can, and will, do their best work with them. If you are working with people with whom you do not do your best work, you are out of integrity.

And as we discussed earlier, you *are* your clients. When your clients go out into the world and speak of you to others, they are representing you.

With whom do you want to be associated—the duds or the ideal clients? It's also the ideal clients, those who are wildly happy with you and your services, who are most likely to go out and talk about you to others, to refer other clients like themselves, more ideal clients. The fewer duds you allow to hang around, the more ideal clients you have room for, the more referrals you'll get, and so on.

Clients are like family to me, so I know this can be hard. I lived through a period of intense and painful negative energy worrying about those challenging client relationships. It exhausted me and took me away from accomplishing the highest good for my clients. It was impossible for me to be productive, effective, or successful when working with less than ideal clients.

Let me share a story with you about myself and my former landscaper, where *I* was the less than ideal client. For a variety of reasons, my landscaper and I were just not a good fit for one another. He had issues with me; he knew I wasn't his ideal client, but rather than tell me so, he stayed with me while getting more and more annoyed until he blew up and acted like a jerk, forcing me to let him go. More than likely, he didn't feel comfortable dumping his dud clients, or the idea had never even crossed his mind. Granted, pruning his dud clients wouldn't have been as easy as pruning his clients' trees, but had he not allowed the situation to deteriorate and end on such a bad note, I might have been able to refer other clients to him who would have been ideal for him. His inability to take the booked solid action step of letting his less than ideal clients go left both of us dissatisfied with the situation and jeopardized his reputation.

This is what can happen when you work with clients who are not ideal for you. At some point, you're going to create a conflict, whether intentionally or not, because you're going to be frustrated with those clients, and those clients will think you're not providing them with good service and they'll be right. It doesn't serve you or the client when you stay in a less than ideal situation. Please don't make the same mistake my landscaper did. If you do, you'll have former clients going out into the world telling anyone who will listen that you're the worst person to work with.

Clients who are not ideal for you are most likely ideal for someone else. There's nothing *wrong* with them, of course. They're just not right for you. So keep in mind that you don't need to fire clients; you just need to help them find a better fit. You can be tactful, diplomatic, and loving. You can even attempt, when appropriate, to refer them to a colleague who might be a better fit. Whenever possible, keep it simple. Try, "I'm not the best person to serve you." Or "I don't think we'd be a good fit."

Are you always going to get a positive response when dumping your dud clients? Probably not. If the first thing that comes to mind is, "I don't want anyone out there thinking badly of me," I'm with you. I want everyone to love me, too. But life can be a complicated experience and you can never please everyone. To even try is an exercise in futility, as the following fable demonstrates.

The Old Man, the Boy, and the Donkey

An old man, a boy, and a donkey were going to town. The boy rode on the donkey and the old man walked beside him. As they went along they passed some people who remarked it was a shame the old man was walking and the boy was riding. The man and boy thought maybe the critics were right, so they changed positions.

Later, they passed some people who remarked, "What a shame! He makes that little boy walk." They then decided they both would walk.

Soon they passed some more people who thought they were stupid to walk when they had a decent donkey to ride. So they both rode the donkey.

Now they passed some people who shamed them by saying how awful to put such a load on a poor donkey. The boy and man said they were probably right, so they decided to carry the donkey. As they crossed the bridge, they lost their grip on the animal, and he fell into the river and drowned.

The moral of the story? *If you try to please everyone, you might as well kiss your ass goodbye.*

Creating Your Red Velvet Rope Policy

The benefits of working with ideal clients are many and meaningful:

- You'll have clean energy to do your best work.
- You'll feel invigorated and inspired.
- You'll connect with clients on a deeper level.
- You'll feel successful and confident.
- You'll know your work matters and is changing lives.
- The magic of you will come to life!

My ideal clients have these qualities:

- Bright (full of light and easily excitable)
- Resilient (keep coming back)
- Courageous (face their fears)
- Think big (their projects benefit large groups of people)
- Value-oriented (they gain value from relationships with me and others)
- Naturally collaborative (they contribute to and focus on their solutions)
- Rapid responders (talk today, done tomorrow)
- Positive (naturally optimistic)

Your list might look completely different. Maybe you only want to work with certain types of clients. Maybe reliability or long-term goals are important to you. Maybe your top priority is how often a client works with you or how many projects they do with you. The economic status of a client may be one factor, but remember—it's only one of many. In fact, it's often a primary consideration for many service professionals who wind up working with clients who are less than ideal. So take heed—the economic status of a potential client should be only one of many considerations. Notice my list above considers the *quality* of my ideal clients first—who they *are* rather than what they *have*.

1.1.4 Written Exercise: Define your ideal client. What type of people do you love being around? What do they like to do? What do they talk about? With whom do they associate? What ethical standards do they follow? How do they learn? How do they contribute to society? Are they smiling, outgoing, creative? What kind of environment do you want to create in your life? And who will get past the red velvet rope policy that protects you? List the *qualities* you'd like your ideal clients to possess.

1.1.5 Written Exercise: Now let's look at your current client base. Whom do you love interacting with the most? Whom do you look forward to seeing? Who are the clients who don't feel like work to you? *Who is it you sometimes just can't believe you get paid to work with?* Write down the names of clients, or people you've worked with, whom you love to be around.

1.1.6 Written Exercise: Get a clear picture of these people in your head. Write down the top five reasons that you love working with them. What about working with them turns you on?

1.1.7 Written Exercise: Now go deeper. If you were working only with ideal clients, what qualities would they absolutely *need* to possess in order for you to do your *best* work with them? Be honest and don't worry about excluding people. Be selfish. Think about yourself. For this exercise, assume you will work only with the best of the best. Be brave and bold and write without thinking or filtering your thoughts.

How different were the last two lists? You may have nailed it the first time. Maybe you're right on track, or maybe you have some perfect client opportunities to uncover.

By knowing who your ideal clients are and selecting only those who have at least 75 percent of the qualities you identified, you will have more fun, accomplish greater results, and experience incredible joy and fulfillment in your business.

This is beneficial because you'll be able to identify other ideal clients you'd love to work with. People enjoy knowing how important they are to you, and if they know you do your best work with, and for, people like them, they are much more inclined to work with you. It raises the stakes for them.

Look at these requirements and think about how you can start to turn them into filters. As for me, I'm like a giant generator—the more gas (meaning projects or clients) I take in, the more power I create. But the wrong kind of fuel causes me to sputter and conk out. Think about a hot sports car running on diesel fuel—not pretty. Neither is this roadster when he gets the wrong kind of energy. Every engine needs a filtration system to keep the system running smoothly and cleanly, just as you need to create a clean system of clients who will filter out the imperfections.

My client filters include these:

- I feel more energized and excited after working with my clients.
- My clients seek open feedback, and better yet, they take action when they get it.
- My clients have faith that leaves some people bewildered and some astonished.
- My clients are not victims; they hold themselves accountable and think about the betterment of others.
- My clients continually seek out and develop valuable personal and professional relationships.
- My clients feel stimulated and energized by the input and collaborative efforts of others.
- My clients use anecdotes and colorful speech, and they share personal stories.
- My clients do not procrastinate; they rapidly respond to new opportunities.
- My clients are naturally optimistic and do not complain.

1.1.8 Written Exercise: What filters do you want to run your perfect clients through?

Ideal Clients, the Duds, and Everyone Else

1.1.9 Written Exercise: Draw a simple table with three columns: Label the first column "Ideal Clients," the second "Duds," and the third "Everyone Else." Now divide your clients into these three groups. Don't hold back.

As you eliminate the duds, you'll open up room for ideal clients. As you use the Book Yourself Solid system to attract more and more ideal clients, you'll discover that you're happier, more vibrant, more energetic, and more productive. You'll be on fire. You'll be giving your clients the best of yourself and your services, and you'll love every minute of it.

As if that weren't enough, you may begin to notice that many of your mid-range clients, those who made neither the ideal client nor the dud list, are undergoing a transformation. Why? While you were working with dud clients, you weren't performing at your best. If you think that wasn't affecting your other clients, think again. The renewed energy and the more positive environment you'll create as a result of letting go of the duds will most likely rejuvenate the relationships between you and some of your mid-range clients, turning many of them into ideal clients.

1.1.10 Written Exercise: Brainstorm your own ideas for reigniting these mid-range clients. Contemplate the ways in which you may, albeit inadvertently, have contributed to some of your clients being less than ideal clients. Are there ways in which you can light a new fire or elicit greater passion for the work you do together? Do you need to set and manage expectations more clearly right from the beginning? Can you enrich the dynamics between you by challenging or inspiring your clients in new ways? Go ahead—turn off your left-brain logical mind for a moment and let your right-brain creativity go wild.

Observe carefully the ways in which your relationships with your clients begin to shift as you embrace the Book Yourself Solid way. Some of your mid-range clients may fall away. Others may step up their game and slide into the ideal client category.

> *When you're fully self-expressed, fully demonstrating your values and your views, you'll naturally attract and draw to yourself those you're best suited to work with, and you'll push away those you're not meant to work with.*

A Perpetual Process

The process we've just worked through is one that you must do on a regular basis. Pruning your client list is a perpetual process because all relationships naturally cycle. The positive and dynamic relationships you have now with your ideal clients may at some point reach a plateau, and the time may come to go your separate ways. You'll get more comfortable with the process over time. It's one that has so many rewards that it's well worth the effort.

I'll let Tom Peters sum it up for us: "This is your life. You *are* your clients. It is fair, sensible, and imperative to make these judgments. To dodge doing so shows a lack of integrity."

I'll go one step further and say that doing so is one of the best and smartest business and life decisions you can make. It's crucial to your success and your happiness. Prune regularly and before you know it you'll be booked solid with clients you love working with.

2

Why People Buy What You're Selling

Before everything else, getting ready is the secret of success.
—Henry Ford

The next few steps we take down the Book Yourself Solid path will either feel like you're skipping over stepping stones or you're taking giant leaps of faith. Either way, these few steps will be well worth the time spent. And please remember to submit to the process. Stay by my side as we walk and work together on getting you booked solid.

Taking the following four steps will help you keenly understand why people buy what you're selling, an essential component in creating relentless demand for your services.

Step 1: Identify your target market.

Step 2: Understand the urgent needs and compelling desires of your target market.

Step 3: Offer investable opportunities.

Step 4: Uncover and demonstrate the benefits of your investable opportunities.

Step 1: Identify Your Target Market

Now that you've looked at the qualities of the people you want to work with, it's time to identify your target market, the specific group of people or businesses you serve. For example, your target market might be seniors or working mothers or service professionals. Your ideal clients are a subset of the target market you choose to serve. It is just as important to identify a target market you feel passionate about as it is to identify the ideal clients you're energized and inspired by. Remember, your ideal clients are those individuals who energize and inspire you; your target market is the demographics of the group you're most passionate about serving.

It's also important to understand the difference between your target market and your niche. If you've done other research or reading on the subject of building your business, you may have heard both of these terms before, and you may have heard them used interchangeably. However, they are *not* the same. There's an important distinction between the two: Your target market is the group of people you serve, and your niche is the service you specialize in offering to your target market. We'll get to your niche in Chapter 3. Before we can talk about the services you offer, you've got to identify your target market.

Even if you believe you have identified and chosen a target market, please don't skip this section. I often see service professionals who are struggling because either they've chosen a target market that isn't as specific as it needs to be, or they've chosen a target market based on what they think is the most logical and most lucrative choice, rather than one they feel passionate about serving. So please read through this section even if you don't think you need to. Trust me. If your target market isn't specific enough or the right one for you, the rest of the book won't be as effective. And besides, you just might be surprised at what you discover.

The ultimate benefit of identifying a target market is that it allows you to more easily determine where to find potential clients who are looking for what you have to offer. This way you know where to concentrate your marketing efforts and what to offer that is compelling and well received.

Marketing and sales isn't about trying to convince, coerce, or manipulate people into buying your services. It's about putting yourself out in front of, and offering your services to, those whom you are meant to serve—people who already need and are looking for your services.

In order to reach the people you're meant to serve, you've got to know where to find them. That's why it's essential for you to identify a very specific target market to serve.

No matter how much you might like to be everything to everyone, it's just not possible. Even if you could be, you would be doing a disservice to yourself and your clients in the attempt. You can serve your clients much better, offer them much more of your time, energy, and expertise, if you narrow your market so that you're serving only those who most need your services and who can derive the greatest benefits from what you have to offer.

If you're just starting out in your business, or if you've been working in your business for a while but are not yet booked solid, you may be tempted to market to anyone and everyone with the assumption that the more people you market to, the more clients you'll get. While it may seem counterintuitive to narrow your market in order to gain more clients, that's exactly what you need to do to successfully book yourself solid.

It's like this: Which would you rather be—a small fish in a big pond or a big fish in a small pond? It's much easier to carve out a very lucrative domain for yourself once you've identified a specific target market. And once you're a big fish in a small pond, you'll get more invitations than you can handle to swim in other ponds.

For example, one of my clients, Dr. Mike Berkley, L.Ac., is a doctor of acupuncture. He specializes in the treatment of male and female infertility using acupuncture and herbal medicine. He's renowned for his work and he's booked solid. In fact, he's overbooked. You'd be lucky to get an appointment with him. Why? Well, he's great at what he does, but he has also chosen a target market that allows him to do his best work, the work that he is most interested in, and which allows potential clients to see him as the answer to their problems.

You might be thinking: "If I specialize and only work with a specific group of people, or specific types of companies within a specific industry, won't that limit my opportunities? And what if I get bored?" Let me answer the second question first. If you're someone who gets bored easily, you may have that problem no matter what you do. You may want to spend some time reflecting on why you're not able to stay focused on what you've chosen to do. Or it may be that you've chosen a target market that doesn't excite you, that you aren't passionate about or interested in.

To answer the first question, once you're booked solid in one target market, if you really want to, you can move into other areas. Dr. Berkley is now also treating postpartum disorders as well as infertility issues. Once he became renowned for his work with infertility, it was easy for him to move into another related and very specific target market. It was precisely because he chose a very specialized target market that he was able to establish himself as an expert, and being known as an expert with one target market made it much easier for him to successfully move into another.

When I started my business, I helped fitness and wellness professionals get booked solid. Once I was fortunate enough to create relentless demand for my services, I expanded my business and began serving other groups of service professionals using my excellent reputation as an expert with fitness and wellness professionals as a springboard into a larger market. I now serve all service professionals. So if you want to increase your speed to getting booked solid, choose a very specific target market and stay with that target market until you are booked solid. Then you can move into other markets if you like.

Your Passions, Natural Talents, and Knowledge Are Key

If you haven't yet chosen a target market, then this is your chance, and I am going to help you. I'm going to ask you to consider what you're most passionate about, what excites you, and what you enjoy doing so much that it feels more like play than work and that will allow you to make the most of your natural talents and your knowledge.

Why start by thinking of your own needs, desires, and passions rather than those of your clients? For one very simple reason: If you are not passionate about what you're doing, if your heart isn't in it, if it doesn't have meaning to you, you are not going to devote the time and energy required to be successful, and you'll never, in a million years, be able to convince people in your target market that you're the best person to help them.

Often when I'm working with clients, I discover they've chosen a target market based on what they think is logical or most lucrative. The end result is that they're bored, frustrated, and struggling to book themselves solid. Don't make that mistake. It is imperative that you work with a target market that excites you, that you can feel passionate about serving. If you don't, growing your business will quickly begin to feel like drudgery, and you'll be miserable. When you choose a target market you're passionate about, growing your business will feel like passionate play and will bring you joy.

Identifying a target market you feel passionate about may sound like a daunting task. Maybe you have the habit of making business decisions based on left-brained, logical thinking. Maybe you're not in the habit of tuning in to your intuition. If this sounds like you, I'm going to ask you to once again set aside any preconceived ideas you may have about how this *should* be done and be open to the possibility that there is another way to make this particular business decision.

Tuning in to your intuition, allowing yourself to open up to new ways of thinking and to the infinite possibilities available to you, may seem illogical, but if you can approach the process I'm about to walk you through with an open mind, you may find that it makes perfect sense.

That's not to say that you shouldn't also consider your clients. If you've been in business for a while, even if you may not have as many clients as you'd like, the clients you do have can help with this process. Look at the clients you're currently serving. Look for common elements among them—for example, a particular industry, geographic location, age, gender, or profession. If you find that most of your clients share one or more common elements, it may be that you are naturally drawn to those elements or they are drawn to you. Perhaps your target market has already chosen you and you just haven't stopped to think about it long enough to realize it and then focus your marketing there.

1.2.1 Written Exercise: Take a few moments to think about the following questions and to jot down whatever comes to you. Doing so will provide you with clues to the target market you're best suited to serve. Your passion, your natural talents, and what you already know and want to learn more about are key.

- Who are all the different groups of people who use the kind of services you provide?
- Which of these groups do you most relate to or feel the most interest or excitement about working with?
- Which group(s) do you know people in or already have clients in?
- Which group(s) do you have the most knowledge about, or on the flip-side, would you find fascinating to learn more about?
- What are you most passionate about as it relates to your work?
- What natural talents and strengths do you bring to your work?
- What aspects of your field do you know the most about?

1.2.2 Written Exercise: Consider your life experience and interests. You'll be able to more sincerely identify and empathize with your target market if you share common life situations or interests.

- What life situations or roles do you identify with that might connect you to a particular target market?
- Do you have any interests or hobbies that might connect you with your target market?

Now that you've given some thought to these questions, are some new possibilities beginning to emerge? Let's take a look at a few examples that might help you to see how you can incorporate some of your answers into serving a target market.

- If you're a graphic designer whose whole family is in the construction industry, maybe you'd choose the construction industry as your target market because you know the sensibilities of the people in that industry, and you know a lot about its inner workings.
- Or perhaps you're a fitness professional and one of your parents suffered from a chronic illness all your life. You know a lot about what it's like to go through that kind of situation and you empathize with and want to help people with chronic illnesses.
- Maybe you're a chiropractor who used to be a semipro athlete and you'd really enjoy working with athletes.
- If you're an accountant and you grew up in a family business that went bankrupt when you were a teen, you might like to work with family businesses to help them avoid what happened to your family.
- If you're a hairstylist who used to be a stay-at-home mom, stay-at-home moms might be a target market you'd relate well to and enjoy working with.
- Perhaps you're a Web designer who is fascinated by—and would like to learn more about—fashion, so you choose the fashion industry as your target market.
- If you're a yoga teacher who loves and naturally connects with children, and you're very creative, imaginative, and patient, you might want to choose children as your target market.

Let's take this last example and examine it more closely. Let's say this yoga teacher is booked solid. Chances are it isn't just because she's an expert on the specific techniques of yoga for children but because she has a natural affinity with children. It's this differentiator that helped her to book herself solid much more quickly than she would have if she focused on serving the general population.

Are you beginning to see the ways in which your passions, natural talents, knowledge, life experience, and even interests and hobbies might help you to choose a more specific target market? Play, explore, and have fun with this process.

1.2.3 Written Exercise: For now I just want you to answer this question: Who is your target market? If you're not ready to make this choice, list the possibilities that appeal to you. Sit with them for a while (but not for too long) and then choose one. Even if you're not sure at this point, it will become clearer to you as you work through the next few chapters.

Remember to tune into your intuition. I can't tell you how many times I've worked with clients who *knew* on some level the target market they most wanted to serve, and for one reason or another discounted it. Turn off your inner censor when doing this exercise and allow yourself to at least explore every possibility, no matter how wild, silly, or unrealistic it may seem on the surface.

Step 2: Identify the Urgent Needs and Compelling Desires of Your Target Market

Your target market's urgent needs and compelling desires prompt them to go in search of you and your services, so it's critical to be able to identify and address them when they come looking or you'll miss your window of opportunity.

> *You must offer what your potential clients want to buy, not what you want to sell or think they should want to buy. You must be able to look at your services from your client's perspective—their urgent needs and compelling desires.*

Your clients' urgent needs are the things they would like to move away from, and their compelling desires are the things that they would like to move toward.

1.2.4 Written Exercise: What are your clients' *urgent needs*? (What are they moving away from?)

Example: The urgent need that may have prompted you to buy this book might be a feeling of stress because you know you need more clients (and more money) but don't know where or how to begin marketing your business. Maybe the bills are really starting to pile up and you're afraid. Or maybe you know what to do to market your services but just aren't doing it. You're procrastinating and your business is suffering as a result.

1.2.5 Written Exercise: What are your clients' *compelling desires*? (What would they like to move toward?)

Example: Let's use you as an example again. Your compelling desire might be to feel confident and in control as you get as many clients as you would like. Maybe you want financial freedom. Maybe you just want to be able to take a real vacation every year. Or maybe it's all about having a thriving business that includes doing what you love and making oodles of money.

Step 3: Offer Investable Opportunities

Do potential clients within your target market see your services and products as opportunities that will give them a significant return on their investment?

They must; if your potential clients are going to purchase your services and products, they *must* see them as investable opportunities; they must feel that the return they receive is greater than the investment they made.

I believe that your clients should be getting a return of at least 20 times their investment in your services. This return will come in different forms, depending on what you offer, but the return is almost always financial or emotional. And the potential return on investment for your clients must be evident before they purchase services from you. When their return is evident, they'll be much more inclined to work with you. If one of my intensive coaching programs requires a financial investment of $1,500, I expect that the average participant will get a return of at least $30,000 in new client business plus personal rewards like increased confidence, focus, total clarity, and more. I'm afraid that sometimes, as service professionals, we forget how important this is. Ask yourself what kind of return on investment a client will get from working with you. Will it be much higher than their financial investment in your services, either in financial returns or emotional returns? If so, how much higher?

Again, I'll use Dr. Mike Berkley of the Berkley Center for Reproductive Wellness as an example. When I started working with him, while his target market was well-defined, he was not positioning his services as investable opportunities. He was selling the features of his services—the science of acupuncture, how it works, how it balances the hormone levels—but he was not making the important *return on investment* connection. He didn't see that he needed to articulate the benefits of his services and the end result his clients would receive. Do you think his potential clients would be more willing to invest in his services if they believed that doing so would substantially increase their chances of conceiving? Of course they would. The truth is that he already had a proven success record. Over 30 percent of his clients can conceive after an average of three months of acupuncture treatment combined with in vitro fertilization (IVF) treatment. Now that's an opportunity that most couples suffering from infertility would be willing to invest in.

The secret to having a successful business is to know what your clients want. So rather than talking about what you do, focus instead on clear, specific, and detailed solutions that solve your clients' problems. People aren't buying what you do. *The science, technique, or technical name that you use won't get clients to hire you!* Clients who understand the distinct benefits and advantages you offer will jump at the chance to work with you. Start by identifying your clients' urgent needs and compelling desires, offer investable opportunities that meet those needs and desires, and you'll be booked solid in no time.

Step 4: Uncover and Demonstrate the Benefits of Your Investable Opportunities

In order to make it obvious that your solutions are investable opportunities for your potential clients, you need to uncover and demonstrate their benefits. The opportunities you offer—acupuncture, financial planning, web site design, career counseling, executive coaching, interior decorating—are just things that you do. They are the actual services you offer; they are *technically* what your clients buy but not what they *actually* buy.

For example, some of my offerings are *technically* these:

- A book that you can read on how to book yourself solid.
- A coaching and training program that teaches you how to book yourself solid.
- Live seminars that teach you how to book yourself solid.

However, these are still only the features and technical offerings. The core benefits of these offerings are much deeper. Benefits are sometimes tangible results, but more often they're intangible; they're the effects your services have on your clients' quality of life. They are what make your offer an investable opportunity. They are what people buy. Don't ever forget that.

To get a stronger sense of how this works, think about this. If I asked you what you wanted to accomplish in the next 90 days, you might say you'd like to get more clients or earn more money, but what is getting more clients really going to give you? Will it give you more than money in the bank or a wallet fat with twenties, fifties, and hundred dollar bills? I'm going to argue that you don't actually want clients or cash. Instead you may want financial freedom, peace of mind, time with your family, or reduced concerns about how you're going to make ends meet. Am I right?

To accentuate this point, here are some more examples of the deeper benefits you'll get from reading this book and participating in my Book Yourself Solid live events and coaching programs:

- A paradigm shift in the way you look at marketing and sales so that you can forever create demand for your services in a way that feels authentic and comfortable to you.
- Increased confidence in yourself and your capacity to handle any business challenge that you are faced with.
- A feeling of pride and a sense of accomplishment as you take the actions you know you need to take and see positive results.
- Freedom from the stress and anxiety of not being able to cover the mortgage for the home you and your children live in.
- And so much more . . .

Do you see how identifying benefits allows you to speak to and touch your target market on a much deeper and more personally and emotionally connected level? The more benefits you uncover, the quicker you will start to attract new clients. People buy results and the benefits of those results. So think about the solutions you offer and the subsequent results and benefits they provide.

1.2.6 Written Exercise: What are the deep-rooted benefits your clients will experience as a result of your services?

Now do you see what clients are actually buying when they decide to work with you? Every time you communicate in person, by writing, on the Internet, in an advertisement, in business meetings, or on the phone, articulate and rearticulate these benefits. Use words that you hear your clients use and express very specific solutions to their very prominent problems.

Even if it seems simple, it's worth repeating. I have a client named Kim who wants to establish her own personal brand and start earning money doing something she loves. Every time we meet, I will remind Kim that her personal brand will offer her freedom so she won't ever have to *settle* again when it comes to the clients she works with. I know that this is an urgent need for her, and I remind her how inspired she is going to feel once she works only with her ideal clients. Keeping the benefits at the top of her mind, Kim clearly sees the fully realized vision of her business and stays focused on accomplishing her goals.

Relax, Be Playful, and Have Fun!

Look for the humor in everything you do and think of ways you can have more fun and help your clients at the same time. Start thinking about how you can incorporate more play into your life and work. Don't be afraid to

- Be playful and quirky—be yourself.
- Be full of energy—enthusiasm is contagious.
- Help others laugh a lot—it's the best sales technique in the world.

It's been said that children laugh an average of 450 times per day, while adults laugh an average of only 15 times a day. If that's true, and based on my experience with my beloved son Jake, it is, how did we end up 435 laughs short of a good time? Embrace a childlike sense of play and you'll be one step closer to booking yourself solid.

Clients Want You to Help Them

Begin to view your role with your clients as that of a highly important and trusted advisor. You have a moral obligation to offer your services to those who need them. To do anything other than counsel, advise, guide, and coach your clients would be a huge disservice. Start to view yourself as a leader in their life.

We all want someone to believe in. Be that person and you can write your own ticket. If you view yourself as a trusted advisor, clients will never forget you. They will come back to you months or even years later. Trust is built over time, so a connection you make today may not develop until much later. Continue to share your vision, mission, and obligation to help people. Give clients benefit after benefit and show them exactly how they can fulfill the promise of your offerings.

There is an acronym that is often used in sales—A, B, C—*always be closing*. Yuck! Sounds like cheesy sales talk to me. Instead, I say—A, B, C— *always be communicating*. Let everybody and anybody know how you help people:

- Whom you serve (your target market).
- What their urgent needs and compelling desires are.
- The investable opportunities you have to offer them.
- What the benefits of your investable opportunities are.

Got it? Good.

Market Research

If you're still struggling with identifying the needs of your target market, doing some market research may be very helpful. Start by identifying other businesses in your field. Then visit their web sites and gather as much information as you can about whom they serve and what solutions they offer. Look for any holes or missing elements in their services that might provide market opportunities for you. If you can provide what others in your field aren't providing, you'll very quickly create a demand for your services. Consider as well whether there are services you could improve upon or unique advantages you can offer to your target market that others can't offer or aren't offering.

Surveys are another great way to identify potential target markets. They provide you with essential information about a broader market's needs and desires. Survey your own clients, clients of other professionals who offer complementary services, visitors to your web site, or members of discussion forums or e-mail groups. It can be helpful to offer some reward or benefit to filling out your survey, such as a discount coupon for services or some other valuable giveaway.

If You Feel Stuck

For some, choosing a target market doesn't come easily. It can feel very challenging, and when you've been told how important it is to identify a target market and it doesn't come quickly and easily, the pressure to choose can feel overwhelming and uncomfortable.

Part of what keeps us stuck is that we take ourselves, and the process, too seriously. We turn it into a big deal and wind up getting more and more frustrated with the whole thing, and with ourselves. Suddenly it's become something to beat ourselves up about. Needless to say, the frustration and self-flagellation just further block our creativity and intuition, and the next thing we know we're in this awful cycle, like a hamster on an exercise wheel spinning around and around and getting nowhere.

So take a few deep breaths and let yourself off the hook. See if you can approach the problem with an attitude of play. Think of it as a jigsaw puzzle—challenging but fun. The point isn't to finish as quickly as possible; the point is to enjoy the process and to find the target market that is right for you.

First you sort through all the pieces to find the edges, the pieces of the puzzle that are easiest to identify and put together. Then you take your time sorting through the rest. You pick one piece up, you compare it to the bigger picture on the box, and you try to figure out where it might go. Gradually, one piece at a time, the puzzle begins to come together. When you get tired or bored or frustrated, or you just feel drawn to do something else, get up and walk away, and as you go about the rest of your day, don't stress out about whether you'll ever get the puzzle finished.

Some days you might spend an hour or two with it, other times only minutes. Maybe every once in awhile you stop for mere seconds, pick up a piece or two, and pop them right in where they fit as you pass by. Maybe a friend or family member stops by for a visit, picks up that piece that's been making you crazy for days, and pops it right into place for you.

Choosing a target market you can feel passionate about serving can be an enjoyable and immensely rewarding process if you approach this process with an open mind and an attitude of play, reaching out for help from family, friends, or a professional business coach to guide you.

Revisit the written exercises in Step 1 of this chapter and approach them with a spirit of play. Don't analyze; just jot down whatever answers come to you. Make it a game, listing as many ideas and possibilities as you can think of. If you're still having difficulty, ask someone to play with you and to offer ideas and suggestions that occur to them, which you may not have the objectivity to consider. Remember to turn your inner censor off for this process. If you need to, let go of the process altogether for awhile and move on. Releasing the pressure of having to choose sometimes allows ideas that were blocked to come racing through.

3

Develop a Personal Brand

Every time you suppress some part of yourself or allow others to play you small, you are in essence ignoring the owner's manual your creator gave you and destroying your design.

—Oprah Winfrey

Branding

Having established your target market and identified the urgent needs and compelling desires of your target market as well as the benefits of the investable opportunities you offer, you are ready to develop a plan for deciding how you want to be known in your market—in a compelling and unforgettable way. You will do this by developing a personal brand. Brands are not just for big corporations. In fact, a personal brand will serve as an important key to your success. A personal brand will help clearly and consistently define, express, and communicate who you are, whom you serve, and why you have chosen to dedicate your life and work to serving your target market so that you can attract your most ideal clients and repel those who are less than ideal. Personal branding is far more than just what you do. It *is* you—uniquely you. It allows you to distinguish yourself and what is unique about who you are and what you do from everyone else.

31

The way I see it, this is about making yourself known for one skill or talent. Master one domain and then you can do just about anything you want. Successful people find their style, build a brand based on it, and boldly express themselves through that brand. It's powerful and it makes you memorable.

Think about some of the most successful people you know. The entertainment industry is a great example. On the television show *In Living Color*, Jim Carrey established himself as a physical comedian using exaggerated body and facial expressions to make us laugh, while Jerry Seinfeld became well known for his intellectual comedic style of observing the obvious. Whoopi Goldberg took an entirely different approach, baring her soul in her standup routines talking about career, motherhood, and the perils of trying to have it all. She used stories and emotions to strike an emotional chord in us to make us laugh. Each of these very different comedic styles is attractive and preferable to different types of people. Some people love Jim Carrey's work, while others don't particularly care for it. The same is true for Jerry and Whoopi. The more bold, authentic, and concise your personal brand is, the more easily you'll attract those you're meant to work with.

That's how a personal brand works—it defines you, but first you must define it. Your personal brand will give you the ability to attract fun and exciting clients who understand and *get* you. And you *get* them. You can see that each of the comedians I described expanded their niche and repertoire after they became well known. Well, all of them except Jerry Seinfeld, who continued in a style that had always been successful for him.

Develop a personal brand that looks like you, thinks like you, sounds and feels like you—one that is instantly recognizable as your essence. It should be:

- Clear
- Consistent
- Authentic
- Memorable
- Meaningful
- Soulful
- Personal

There are two components to your personal brand. The first is your *who and do what* statement, which is based on:

- Specific problems you solve.
- Who you solve them for.
- What the results are.

The second is your *why you do it* statement, and it's based on:

- Who you are at your core.
- Why you do what you do.
- Why people should work with you.

Releasing Blocks

Before we begin to craft your personal brand, it's important to address any blocks you may be inadvertently creating that may hold you back from achieving success. I know it may seem unusual to discuss personal blocks as it relates to personal branding, but as I learned from Dave Buck of Coachville.com, most business problems are really personal problems in disguise. The following questions can help you gain clarity about how you want to be known in the world. Consider them seriously.

> *The greatest strategy for personal and business development on the planet is bold self-expression.*

Are you fully self-expressed? Again, I know this may seem like an unusual question. But I ask it because in order to create a gutsy, passionate, ardent, provocative, courageous, valiant, vibrant, dynamic, luminous, and respected personal brand, you must be fully self-expressed. You can't hide behind the shingle that you've hung over your door and you can't water yourself down in any way, shape, or form. If you do, you won't be of interest to the people you're meant to serve.

Michael Gerber, in his best-selling *The E-Myth: Why Most Businesses Don't Work and What to Do About It*, makes the distinction between working *on* your business—creating the framework that supports the business itself, such as setting up an automatic marketing system—and working *in* your business, which means working with the clients you serve. If I may be so presumptuous as to add one more element to Gerber's profound message: We must also work on ourselves. How we brand ourselves is a reflection not only of how we want to be known but also of our ability to work *on* our business, while working *in* our business and *on* ourselves.

Have you compromised yourself or watered yourself down in any area of your business? For example, have you been in a business situation where you walked away feeling like you settled for less or compromised your integrity? You may be thinking, "I don't sell out. I've never compromised or sold out." If you haven't, you are unique. It's completely normal to compromise yourself or to be out of integrity from time to time. We all are.

It will serve you well to know exactly where you have run into trouble in the past. Since working independently and starting and running your own business is really challenging, you can eliminate a lot of pain and surprise right now by acknowledging the issues you may have buried or have had a difficult time confronting in the past.

1.3.1 Written Exercise: List the ways in which you've sold out, settled for less, or compromised your integrity in your business, either now or in the past.

1.3.2 Written Exercise: What about the flip-side? Tap into instances in your business life where you've felt alive and vibrant—fully self-expressed. Everything you did just flowed. Draw on all of your senses. What was happening at that time that made you feel so alive?

1.3.3 Written Exercise: Now compare the two areas, the ones where you sold out and the situations where you felt most fully self-expressed. How can you change your behavior to speak boldly and from a place of free-expression so that you're working in situations that make you feel fully self-expressed? How will you communicate to make sure you stop compromising or watering yourself down in the future?

1.3.4 Written Exercise: Start with a few situations (fairly comfortable ones) in which you could practice speaking from a bolder and more self-expressed place.

1.3.5 Written Exercise: Write down a few more situations (that seem a little more difficult) that you'd like to work up to speaking more boldly about.

There are two reasons for the exercises you're doing. The first is so you can help clients understand how you can help them. The second is so you can make sure that your personal and professional intentions are clear.

As I learned from Dave Buck, clear intentions allow you to gracefully and confidently move toward your goals. Conflicting intentions will undermine your success without your even knowing it. They will hold you back from your dreams. They are the mother of energy-drain and confusion. Anthony Robbins, author of *Unlimited Power*, calls the personal battle of conflicting intentions, "inner civil war." From a perspective of personal brand identity, conflicting intentions will eventually lead to a bland message and a less successful you.

Here's a story to illustrate this concept. My father is a highly accomplished psychiatrist. I have always had great respect for him and his work. And, above all, I've always wanted him to be proud of me and my accomplishments. That's natural, right?

When I first launched my service business, I spent lots of time getting clear on my offerings and how I would communicate them to the world.

And then I did just that—or so I thought. I let everybody know what I was up to. However, not too much was happening. I got a few clients, but as I mentioned earlier, I couldn't really pay the bills, and I certainly wasn't happy with the response I was getting. So a few months later, when I was at my wits' end, I did a formal evaluation of my brand. I started with my web site. I locked myself away and read every word on my web site from start to finish. I sat back in my chair, staring at the screen in amazement and shock. The entire feeling of the site was not really me—it was almost as if my father were talking. In fact, I was communicating what I thought he would approve of.

I am not my father. I'm certainly not a medical doctor. Not having his credentials, I shied away from being bold and brave and instead played it safe, secretly hoping that he would approve of what I was doing. The reason this is relevant is that when I started my business, I was focusing more on personal development issues—what some might call Life Coaching. I wanted to help people become happier and more successful. So I had two very conflicting intentions. One intention was to build a wildly successful business and the second (my conflicting intention) was to make my father proud. The underlying dynamic was not to do anything that he wouldn't approve of. But remember what I mentioned earlier: Most business problems are personal problems in disguise.

Even now, as a business coach and consultant, much of the work I do is centered on helping people move through personal problems so they can be successful in business. I'm not practicing psychology by any stretch of the imagination. However, I often relate to people on a very deep level. By remaining within conventional boundaries—the ones that I *thought* my father would approve of—I limited myself dramatically. I didn't give myself the freedom to be truly me. I was inhibited and unable to offer the full extent of my experiences, point of view, and passion. The result was a rather confusing and bland identity. And the truth is, I had no proof or real reason to believe that my father wouldn't approve of my being authentically me. In fact, just the opposite is true; he wouldn't want me to be anyone but me. It was just a good story for me to hide behind.

In order to set clear intentions for yourself, you must remove the conflicting intentions that you currently have. Your reality is created by your present intentions. If you want to change your reality, you must change your intentions. My vision for you is that, through this book, the intentions for your life and your business will become more clear to you and to your clients.

1.3.6 Written Exercise: Identify one of your most important intentions as it relates to your business.

Example: I intend to book myself solid.

1.3.7 Written Exercise: Take a good hard look within to see if you can identify any potentially conflicting intentions for the intention you identified. These are likely to be subconscious and more difficult to identify, and they are nearly always fear based.

Example: If I book myself solid I won't have time for myself. Or, in order to book myself solid, I'll have to promote myself, and self-promotion will make me feel pathetic and vulnerable. Or maybe you want to book yourself solid but you *think* self-promotion is unattractive.

1.3.8 Booked Solid Action Step: Identifying and acknowledging your conflicting intentions is the first big step in releasing them. Awareness is key, but not always enough to prevent conflicting intentions from affecting and blocking our positive intentions. The next step in the process is to identify the underlying fears. Once you've identified them, you can begin to take steps to relieve them.

For this step it's critical that you very carefully choose one or two sincerely and highly supportive friends to share your new insights with. They must be truly supportive and willing to help you change. Often as we begin to make changes in our lives, whether business or personal, some of our most dearly loved friends and family can feel threatened by the process of change. While they may consciously want you to be successful, they may have their own subconscious conflicting intentions and be highly invested in wanting to maintain their own comfort zone by keeping you in yours. These are not the folks you want to ask for help with this exercise.

(Continued)

> Share the intentions and their conflicting counterparts with one or two others and ask your friends to help you in recognizing whether these are genuine concerns or unfounded fears. Then brainstorm ways to address the problems.
>
> While you can take this step on your own, often we're too close to our own fears to see them clearly. Having a supportive friend, mentor, or professional coach who has a bit more objectivity than we do can help to put them in perspective.

You Are Uniquely You

Often it's those qualities that make you uniquely you—the ones that come so naturally to you that you don't even think about them—that become the best personal brands. Susan's story illustrates the point.

A few years ago, Susan, a pleasant woman in her early forties, came to me and asked me to help her discover "what she was born to do" so she could launch her own business. It was a particularly tough time for her. She had recently been divorced and needed to support herself. As you might imagine, she was concerned about what she would do. Years earlier she had been a successful trader on Wall Street. Yet it had now been over 20 years since her glory days. I asked her, "What are your quirks?" "Quirks?" she replied. "I don't have any quirks." She sounded moderately offended. "Okay," I said, "Then tell me about your friendships; what are they based on?" Without a moment's hesitation she said, "My female friends are always asking me for advice on sex and intimacy." "Interesting. Now we're getting somewhere," I thought.

She told me about her unusual habit of giving scarlet-colored thongs (not the ones of the flip-flop variety) as gifts. Remember, this is the same woman who told me she didn't have any quirks. After more prodding and investigating this unique, special, and entertaining quirk, it became clear that she was fully self-expressed when she was thinking and focusing on how women 40 and over can be, should be, and are, remarkable sexual beings (and more). She decided, even though she would have to resolve many conflicting intentions about doing so, that she was going to exploit her quirk and create *The Scarlet Thong Society*, a social club for women over 40 who want to acknowledge their sexual prowess.

You may not have scarlet thongs to hand out, but chances are you do have something unique, maybe even quirky, that you really want to express and that others will notice and respond to.

1.3.9 Written Exercise: To know which secret quirk or natural talent is waiting in the wings to bring you wealth, happiness, and unbridled success in your business, answer the following questions:

- How are you unique?
- What are three things that make you memorable?
- What are the special talents that you are genetically coded to do? What have you been good at since you were a kid?
- What do people always compliment you on?
- What do you love or never grow tired of talking about in your personal life?
- What do you want to say that you would never grow tired of talking about when you are asked about your work?

Many times we are too close to see the qualities or quirks that stand out to others. Send a few of these questions to different people in your life to get their responses about you and your personality. Not only will you start to see some of the same truths about who you are, but you'll get back the most touching and warm e-mails—I promise. Try it.

1.3.10 Booked Solid Action Step: Send an e-mail to five or more people (include friends, family, clients, neighbors, and acquaintances from all the different aspects of your life).

- Ask them to provide you with your top five personality traits or quirks.
- Ask for fun or unique experiences they've had with you.
- Tell them to be brave and not to be shy.

Remember that your work is doomed to fail if you don't love it and share it with the world. And here's the biggie: *When you're fully self-expressed, you will love marketing.* You won't have conflicting intentions about promoting yourself. You won't feel that the world is coming to an end when you get a rejection. You'll smile and move on to the next opportunity because your ability to express yourself is directly proportional to your level of confidence and vice versa.

With all of this new and insightful information about yourself, you should be thrilled that you've already made it through the challenge of choosing your path and being an independent business owner. That's no easy task. Keep all of these insights in mind as you begin to craft your own personal brand.

The Two Components of Your Personal Brand

As I mentioned at the beginning of this chapter, there are two components to your personal brand:

1. Your *who and do what* statement.
2. Your *why you do it* statement.

I want you to laser-beam your focus on these two aspects of your personal brand until you feel totally and utterly fully expressed when you put words to your *who and do what* and your *why you do it* statements. The process may take a week or it may take a few months. It took me six months. The important thing is to give yourself the time to really give thought to it all.

Your Who and Do What *Statement*

Your *who and do what* statement lets others know exactly whom you help and what you can help them do. It is the first filter that people will put you through when considering your services for hire. Your potential clients will look at it to see if you help people in their specific situation.

1.3.11 Written Exercise: Start with the basics. Keep it simple and straightforward. What is your *who and do what* statement? Whom do you help and what do you help them do? Refer to your target market from Chapter 2. The first time around, just come up with something accurate and clear for now. List as many possibilities as come to mind. Finish this statement, "I help . . ."

Example: I help . . . professional service providers book themselves solid.

Your **Why You Do It** *Statement*

Many others in your industry will share your *who and do what* statement. That's why, after potential clients identify with your *who and do what* statement, they will want to know if they connect with you on an emotional or philosophical level. They'll want to know if they connect with your *why you do it* statement—the reason you do what you do. It's your job to make sure they understand exactly why you're the person to serve their very specific, and personal, urgent needs and compelling desires. Those who resonate with your *why you do it* statement will feel it on a deep level and be strongly, almost magnetically, attracted to you. That will be the defining moment they need to decide whether to purchase your services, products, or programs.

In my business, I am known as "the guy to call when you're tired of thinking small." This is no accident; I've been saying this over and over since the day I realized that being "the guy to call when you're tired of thinking small" was my *why I do it* statement. It's based on the reason I do what I do—to help people think bigger about who they are and what they offer the world.

Your *why you do it* statement is something you'll never get tired of. And the first time you hear someone refer to you by it, you'll want to cry tears of joy. I formulated one simple sentence that allows people to define me in a manner of my own choosing. I never get tired of saying it or hearing it because I really want people to think big, not only about who they are but about what they offer others. And most important, not only does it very deeply and truly mean something to me but it resonates with the people I'm meant to serve.

Your *why you do it* statement lets others know what it's like to be around you. It says something about who you are at your core, and it's the essence of what you want to achieve in the world. It's the bigger vision that is the inspiration for what you do in your business. It's the way in which you want to touch others' lives in a positive and meaningful way.

You may have noticed that my *why I do it* statement is much bigger than my *who and do what* statement. It may resonate with many people; professional service providers aren't the only ones who want to think bigger about who they are and what they offer the world. But I've chosen to offer my services to this inspired group of people, not to every single soul on the planet. Your *why you do it* statement is not about your target market; it's about the emotional connection you make with people. Many people serve the same target market you serve, but your *why you do it* statement is what will resonate with some people and not with others: It will resonate with those you're meant to serve.

Why have you dedicated your life to serving others? How do you want to make a difference?

If you don't want to make a difference, consider making your living as something other than a service professional. The operative word is service.

1.3.12 Written Exercise: It's time to step out of your comfort zone again. Set aside that inner critic and give yourself permission to think big—I mean really *big*, bigger than you've ever dared to think or dream before. Be your most idealistic, inspired, creative, powerful you. What is your purpose? What is your vision of what you hope to achieve through your work? Remember, your work is an expression of who you are. List whatever comes to mind.

1.3.13 Written Exercise: Keeping the above in mind, craft a minimum of three possible *why you do it* statements.

1.3.14 Booked Solid Action Step: If your *why you do it* statement is not immediately and easily identifiable, get together with a group of supportive friends or associates who know you well and ask them to brainstorm it with you. Often it's the things about you that are most natural and that you don't even recognize that become key elements of your *why you do it* statement. Having some outside input and a few more objective perspectives can make all the difference.

Roma Non è Stata Construita in un Giorno (Rome Wasn't Built in a Day)

Neither was my personal brand. I went through many, many versions, even one a month, before I got to a *why I do it* statement that worked for me. I didn't get caught up in trying to find the perfect brand message or positioning statement. I didn't worry about it because I knew I could change it. I knew that creating a statement was a process and that I'd just keep changing it until I got there. If I didn't start with something, though, what would I have had? I'd have had nothing.

First I got clear on my *who and do what* statement, that "I help professional service providers get more clients."

What took longer was to get my philosophical *why I do it* statement. I worked really hard on trying to find mine. It took about six months. I thought about it every day, but the amazing thing was that it came to me by accident. I was with a bunch of people and we were masterminding and brainstorming about our businesses and everyone was talking about what they did. I was giving the others a hard time, teasing and questioning, asking, "Why would I hire you for that?" I was playing the Devil's advocate until finally, one of the women gave it right back to me and said, "Yeah, well why would I hire you?" I blurted out, "Because I'm the guy to call when you're tired of thinking small." Suddenly the whole room went silent, as if everyone was holding their breath. After a few moments the same woman shouted out "Yes! That is *so you!*" Everyone in the room was cheering and the air was charged with excitement.

Even so, I didn't really think much about it until a couple of weeks later as I was talking to a colleague about creating The Think Big Revolution (www.ThinkBigRevolution.com), a place where people could gather online to think bigger about who they are and what they offer the world. I was excited about it, but I questioned it: "I'm not sure about this *big* stuff. I came up with this brand positioning statement that I'm 'the guy to call when you're tired of thinking small,' but I'm not sure about it. What's the big deal about that?" She laughed and said, "Michael, are you dense?" I said, "Yes, but you're going to have to be more specific." She explained to me that she likes being around me because I help her think so much bigger about who she is and what she offers the world.

I realized then that because it was so natural to me to want to help people think bigger about who they are and what they offer the world, it didn't seem like such a big deal to me. It took discussing it with others who weren't as close to it as I was to get the perspective I needed. The exact thing that came most naturally to me was the thing that was drawing people to me, instilling in them the desire to purchase my products and enroll in my programs and seminars.

As I began using my *why I do it* statement to let others know why I do what I do, I found that the people for whom it resonated would immediately comment on how much they connected with it. Those who didn't *get* it, like one of my college friends, would ask me, "What's this silliness about being the guy to call when you're tired of thinking small?" That's okay. It's all about attracting those people who are meant to work with you. The rest will be attracted to someone with whom they will resonate, and you won't end up with less than ideal clients.

Recall the story about the old man, the boy, and the donkey. The process of booking yourself solid isn't about how to please as many people as possible. It's about how to convey your own unique message to those who are waiting to hear it. That can't be achieved with personal branding that's been watered down in an attempt to appeal to everyone. It can be achieved only through bold, no-holds-barred self-expression. It's about being uniquely you.

4

How to Talk About What You Do

A conversation is a dialogue, not a monologue. That's why there are so few good conversations: due to scarcity, two intelligent talkers seldom meet.

—Truman Capote

A primary reason that many service professionals fail to build thriving businesses is that they struggle to articulate—in a clear and compelling way—exactly what solutions and benefits they offer.

Over the course of this chapter, I'm going to teach you the Book Yourself Solid Dialogue, a creatively prepared conversation that will spark curiosity and interest about you and your services, products, and programs. The Book Yourself Solid Dialogue will allow you to have a meaningful conversation with a potential client or referral source. It's a dynamic, lively description of the people you help, what challenges they face, how you help them, and the results and benefits they get from your services. It is intended to replace the static, boring, and usual response to the question, "What do you do?" The typical response is, "I'm a business consultant," or "I'm a massage therapist," or "I'm a graphic designer." Unfortunately, a polite nod or comment, or worse yet, an awkward silence and a completely blank stare follow. Once you get that response, anything more you say about yourself or your services is likely to sound pushy.

Instead you'll learn the Book Yourself Solid way to create a meaningful, connected *dialogue* with a potential client or referral source. Think of it as a conversation between two people each of whom actually cares about what the other has to say. The beautiful thing is that it's based on successfully understanding why people buy what you're selling. And because of the work we did together in Chapter 2, you already know why people buy what you're selling.

You previously created your *who and do what* statement. That's a fantastic first step and an excellent tool for starting a conversation about what you do. Now you must be sure that you can captivate and actively engage the person you're talking to in a conversation that elicits questions rather than just polite acknowledgment. You must talk *with* people, not *at* them. Never give anyone a prepared script because doing so is a train wreck waiting to happen. The long, medium, and short version of your Book Yourself Solid Dialogue will allow you to have conversations with different people in different situations, so you're always prepared. You tell them about the people you work with and then you let them respond. You respond again and before you know it, you are having a conversation that is informative and inspiring—and that's the key to talking about what you do without being bland or confusing.

We hear the question "What do you do for a living?" all the time. Your professional category is the wrong answer.

You are so much more than your profession. Let's toss out the generic labels for now. Teacher, doctor, designer, accountant, acupuncturist, personal fitness trainer, yoga teacher, consultant, coach, or other bland description defines you as one of the masses.

Think about it for a second. Let's say you're a yoga teacher and you meet someone who really needs your help who would also be an ideal client. The only problem is that she has a preconceived notion of what yoga is all about and what a yoga teacher is like, and it's not a preconceived notion that sets you up for success.

Imagine this scenario: The potential client asks you what you do. You say, "I'm a yoga teacher." Before you know what's happened, you see the potential client's face contort, her left eyebrow lifts along with the left side of her upper lip, and her nostrils begin to flare. The potential client says, "Oh, yeah . . . I had a yoga teacher as a neighbor once. She was really weird and made my life miserable. In fact, I had to move out of that apartment because of her and I loved that apartment! She had scores of people coming in and out at all hours of the day, blasting strange music and chanting like the world was about to end—I think they must have been members of a cult. Oh, and you wouldn't believe the awful smell that I was subjected to from the perpetual cloud of incense that invaded my home."

Uh-oh.

Would you like to get that kind of response when you tell someone what you do? And this can happen to any service professional, not just to a yoga teacher. Say a stock broker meets someone whose only introduction to stock brokers has been the movie *Boiler Room* (a movie that came out in 2000 about stock brokers who try to swindle innocent people out of their life's savings). Not a pretty picture.

How much more are you than your professional title? Your Book Yourself Solid Dialogue will allow you to set yourself apart from everyone else whose professional title is the same as yours. It provides you with the opportunity to highlight the ways in which you and your services, products, and programs are unique—and do so with passion.

What's in It for Me?

The greatest breakthroughs in your business will come when you find out on a very deep and personal level exactly what your clients need. Don't just look to the first layer of problems. Go further. Find out what they are really looking for. Ask yourself these questions: What is the deeper problem? What do they really want? What results do they want to achieve? How will their life be intrinsically better once they start working with me? These are the things that will grab the attention of those you're speaking with.

If your Book Yourself Solid Dialogue reads like your resume, you'll bore people to tears, and although they may not say it, they'll be thinking, "Who cares? So what? What has any of that got to do with me?" Your potential client wants to know: "What's in it for me?"

Developing Your Book Yourself Solid Dialogue

We're going to break this down into its smallest components and gather all the information we've worked hard to compile in the previous pages. You've chosen your target market and you've begun to develop your personal brand by crafting your *who and do what* statement and your *why I do it* statement. Now we're going to go back through all the exercises you've done and clean up your core message. If you've kept up on the exercises, crafting your Book Yourself Solid Dialogue will be a relatively simple process, and yet this powerful piece will make all the difference in your business and your message.

Five-Part Book Yourself Solid Dialogue Formula

Let's put it all together and create a few different versions of your Dialogue: long, medium, and short. You've already done the majority of the work to craft a meaningful and connected Book Yourself Solid Dialogue.

1.4.1 Written Exercise: Each of the following five parts has already been answered in previous exercises. All you need to do is pull the pieces into the formula below. The examples are in script format that you can use as a template. Let's get started.

Part I: Summarize your target market in one sentence.

Part II: Identify and summarize the three biggest and most critical problems that your target market faces.

Part III: List how you solve these problems and present clients with unique solutions.

Part IV: Include the most dramatic ("Wow!") results that you or your clients have achieved.

Part V: List the results and deepest benefits your clients receive.

The Long Version

All you need to do is insert parts one through five from Written Exercise 1.4.1 into the following formula:

- You know how [insert Part I] do, are, or feel [insert Part II]?
- Well, what I do is [insert Part III].
- The result is [insert Part IV].
- The benefits are [insert lots of Part V].

You now have an outline that will help you clearly articulate what you do without sounding confusing and bland. In fact, you'll sound like a superstar because you can use this outline or framework to have a meaningful conversation with another human being. Don't stay married to the format, though. Make sure you're improvisational. You may not need to go through every element of this framework in every conversation. The person you're engaged with might end up doing all the talking and even supply your side of the dialogue accurately. Then you can just sit back and relax. The point is, if you're armed with all of these elements, you have the required ingredients for talking about what you do so you can cook up a sweet and tasty business, booked solid with high-paying, high-value clients.

Example: Here is how my very long version goes. (Make note of how each part of the exercises you've just done fits into the dialogue, and note also how each part flows as the result of a natural conversation.)

Setting: Casual conversation at a cocktail party

JOE: Hey, Michael, what is it that you do?

MP: Thanks for asking, Joe. You know how many self-employed professionals (Part I) go out on their own looking for the freedom that working independently promises but they wind up isolated, frustrated, and often struggling financially? (Part II) Do you know people like that?

JOE: Oh, yeah, I definitely do. Actually, that sounds exactly like my sister, Jane.

MP: Oh, no kidding . . . is she working more hours than she should or wants to, never seems to be able to relax, and is constantly stressed about money? Or worse . . . has she become disillusioned about working for herself (more of Part II)?

JOE: Yeah, that's exactly right! I've been trying to encourage her, but frankly I'm all out of ideas as to how to help her.

MP: I hear you. I totally understand you. Please tell her that she's not alone. Her situation is remarkably common. So common, in fact, that I teach a system for service professionals to book themselves solid in my live seminars and coaching programs (Part III). Fortunately, over ninety percent of the people who have gone through my programs increase the number of clients they serve by over 34 percent and improve their revenues by over 42 percent (Part IV). So, there's hope!

JOE: Oh, wow! That's pretty cool.

MP: Well, yeah, it's very cool, and it's about more than just getting clients and making money. My clients begin to think a heck of a lot bigger about who they are and what they offer the world. They are finally free from stressful financial worries and are able to passionately share their work with the people they're meant to serve (Part V).

Joe sighs, takes a meaningful pause, then says . . .

JOE: I'm so glad I asked you what you did. How can I get my sister in touch with you? She could really use your help.

MP: Yes, and I'm so thankful to have had the opportunity to talk about how I could help your sister. Here's my card. All my info is on it, but why don't you give me your sister's e-mail address and I'll send her a personal note telling her how we know each other and that you thought I could be of service to her. I'll copy you on the e-mail as well.

JOE: That would be great, Michael. This way I don't have to put it on my already overly long to-do list.

MP: You know, I wrote a book based on my system called *Book Yourself Solid*. I believe I have a copy in the car. Why don't I go and get it for you. You can give it to your sister as a gift.

JOE: That would be great, thanks. I'll come with you!

Michael and Joe continue their conversation as they walk out to Michael's car.

That's a pretty good way to have a real conversation with someone about what you do.

The Mid-length Version

You can easily adapt the Book Yourself Solid Dialogue as needed. Try a mid-length version and just tighten it up a bit.

- You know how [insert Parts I and II]?
- Well, what I do is [insert Parts III and V].

Example: The mid-length version of my Book Yourself Solid Dialogue goes something like this (remember, conversations never go the same way twice).

Setting: Industry conference

LISA: Nice to meet you, Michael. What do you do for a living?

MP: Thanks for asking, Lisa. You know how many small business owners are always looking to find more clients but complain that they
hate marketing and selling (Parts I and II)?

LISA: I sure do, Michael. I'm one of those business owners, and I always
need new clients, but I really hate marketing and selling!

MP: Well, what I do is teach people like you how to love marketing and
selling, and at the same time, get as many clients as their heart desires (Part III and V).

LISA: Wouldn't that be great! How do you do that?

And now we're really talking!

Short and Sweet

Now go for the short version, which is essentially your *who and do what*
statement.

- I help [Part I] . . . [insert Part V].

Example: Here's how my short version might go.

Setting: Checkout line at the supermarket

BOBBY: Nice to meet you, Michael. What do you do?

MP: I help professional service providers—health and wellness professionals, financial planners, consultants, and others (Part I)—market
and sell their services so they can book as many clients as they
would like (Part V).

BOBBY: Oh, that's very interesting. My wife has a home-based business.
Can you help her?

MP: Tell me a bit about what she does and what kind of support you think she needs.

Again, now we're in real conversation.

Or you can go back to the way you've always done things and say, "Hi, I'm [your name here]. I'm a [add professional title]." Not quite the same impact and more than likely the end of the conversation.

Once you've clearly identified your target market, understand their needs and desires, and can articulate how you help them by identifying the core benefits associated with the results of your services, you'll never be caught off guard again. I suggest you continue to hone and refine your message and then practice over and over. I do.

Getting into a Book Yourself Solid Dialogue with Ease

Start in the comfortable confines of your home; it may take some time for your Book Yourself Solid Dialogue to feel natural. While you don't want your dialogue to sound stiff and rehearsed, you do want to practice it. The more you practice it, the more comfortable you'll get with it and the less rehearsed it will sound. Before long you should be able to recite it in your sleep. You only get one chance to make a first impression. Present yourself and your business in a powerful and compelling way.

Practicing in this way will help you to become comfortable with the multitude of ways in which your Book Yourself Dialogue will unfold when you're speaking with a variety of people. It is truly a dialogue, not a speech or script, so every time you have a dialogue with someone about what you do, it will be unique. Since the people you'll be speaking with won't be reading a script, they may or may not respond in similar ways to what I've outlined above, but you'll soon discover that when you know your Book Yourself Solid Dialogue well, it won't matter. You'll easily and effortlessly respond in the most appropriate way.

1.4.2 Booked Solid Action Step: Practice with a colleague or two. Call one another spontaneously to ask, "What is it that you do?" If you're afraid you'll choke when answering the phone and unexpectedly hear that question, then put your Book Yourself Solid Dialogue up on the wall by the phone as a reminder. The most important principle of the Book Yourself Solid system is actually using what I teach you. Learning it is only a means to an end. Taking action will get you booked solid.

After you've practiced with your colleague, answer these questions for one another:

- Did I sound relaxed and comfortable?
- Could you sense my passion and excitement for what I do?
- What really grabbed your attention?
- What did you like best/least about my Book Yourself Solid Dialogue?

Use this exercise as the great opportunity it is to get honest, open feedback so that you can fine-tune your Book Yourself Solid Dialogue and make it the best it can be.

Tell Everyone You Know

Don't just use the Book Yourself Solid Dialogue when you speak with potential clients. Talk to everyone you know and meet because everyone knows someone who could potentially work with you. When you share this clear understanding of what you do and the problems that you solve, other people will get excited with and for you—and potentially want to refer people to you.

It's More Than Just Words—The 55/38/7 Rule

There are so many different ways to articulate your message. Don't just depend on your words to do it. How you communicate goes far beyond the spoken message. Dr. Albert Mehrabian, a communications researcher at the University of California, Los Angeles, reported in his book, *Silent Messages—*

which was based on extensive clinical experiments on communication, attitudes, likes, and dislikes—that 55 percent of the way that people respond to you is based mostly on facial cues, 38 percent is based on your tone, and only 7 percent is based on what you say—the information you provide.

Speak from the Heart

Be sure to speak with lots of expression. Get excited and show the passion you have for the problems you solve and what you do in the world. If you're not very interested in what you do, no one else will be.

> *When you're passionate and excited about what you do and you let it show, it's incredibly attractive. Real passion can't be faked and there's nothing more appealing and convincing than knowing someone is speaking from the heart.*

And don't forget to:

- *Smile.* I mean really smile—a big, bold, friendly smile.
- *Make eye contact.* You can't connect with others on a deep level if you aren't making eye contact.
- *Be confident.* Use confident, open body language. Stand up straight yet relaxed.
- *Listen!* Stop and listen intently to the needs and desires of the person you're speaking to so that you can address whatever is most important and relevant to them.

A well-crafted Book Yourself Solid Dialogue that is delivered with ease and sincerity and infused with your own unique brilliance and passion is incredibly powerful. Claim your passion, claim your voice, and share it with the world one person at a time.

Building Trust
and Credibility

To be booked solid requires that you are considered credible within your marketplace, that you be perceived as likeable, and that you earn the trust of the people you'd like to serve. Now that you've got a solid foundation, it's time to look at how to develop a strategy for creating trust and credibility so that you stand out from the crowd and begin to build relationships with your potential clients. Your strategy will be based on:

- Becoming and establishing yourself as a likeable expert in your field.
- Building relationships of trust over time through your sales cycle.
- Developing brand-building products and programs.
- Having sincere sales conversations that get results.

In the first module you spent time contemplating the people you want to serve, how best to serve them, how to express yourself uniquely through the services you offer, and how to talk to people you hope to serve about how you can help them. Now it's time to step things up a notch and look at what you have to do, be, and create to begin reaching out to the people you're meant to serve.

As before, I'll walk you step-by-step through the process and you'll begin to see that marketing and sales doesn't have to be so hard after all. In fact, I think you'll find that it can even be exciting and fun.

5

Who Knows What You Know and Do They Like You?

I am not young enough to know everything.

—Oscar Wilde

Have you heard the expression, "It's not what you know that's important but who you know"? It's only partially true. If you're a professional service provider, it's "Who knows *what* you know?" and "Do they *like* you?" that's important. So it's time to establish yourself as a category authority—a well-known, well-liked expert in your field.

But before we discuss how to position yourself as an expert within your field, let's get down to the nitty-gritty—the standard credibility builders. The standard credibility builders are the things that you need to do and have in place to appear credible and professional. Once you have all your basics covered, then and only then can we discuss how to establish your reputation as an authority within your category and look at how your likeability influences your ability to get booked solid.

The Standard Credibility Builders

The standard credibility builders may seem obvious, but without them you won't be taken seriously, so they're worth reviewing:

- *You must have a professional e-mail address,* preferably one that includes your domain name. juicytushy@aol.com doesn't qualify. Neither does 175bb3c@yahoo.com. If you don't yet have a web site, then at least use your name: johndoe@aol.com.
- *Invest in quality business cards.* Business cards with perforated edges that you've printed at home, or the free cards with the printing company's name on the back, will undermine your credibility.
- *If you don't have a web site, have one built now!* Actually, wait until you read Chapter 12, the Book Yourself Solid Web Strategy. If you do have a web site and it's out of date or created using a free template, build a new one. Please don't use templates—unless they are out of this world. If you're in business for yourself, have a professional design your site. Nothing will detract from your credibility more than having a web site that is gathering flies on the Net.
- *Have professionally produced photographs taken.* Display them on your web site and in promotional materials. A photo of you in your pj's with your cat is not going to inspire a lot of confidence (unless, of course, you own a pet store that also sells pajamas). Find any way you can to use pictures or video to demonstrate your professionalism on all promotional materials both online and off. When you're at seminars, have your picture taken with other well-known professionals within your industry and use them in your promotional materials. And certainly display photographs of yourself speaking to groups of people or engaged with your customers and clients. Not having a photograph readily available on your web site or marketing materials leaves your potential clients wondering what you have to hide and doesn't give them the opportunity to connect with you.
- *Obtain and showcase specific testimonials rather than general testimonials.* A comment from a client named H.G. that says, "Pam was great. She

really helped" is not going to hold a lot of weight and it's certainly not going to get you booked solid. However, a very specific testimonial from a person with a name, a company, and maybe even a web site address, if applicable, that says, "In two months, Pam helped me lose fifteen pounds. I could not have done it without her!" will hold weight (no pun intended). It is results oriented. If Pam is a nutritionist, this kind of testimonial will represent the results that many of her clients want to achieve. Even better would be a highly recognized testimonial. For example, if Cindy Crawford was a client of Pam's and she offered the same testimonial, wouldn't you want to work with Pam? You'd figure, if she's good enough for Cindy, she's good enough for you. I would. This is important because these days testimonials have become rather routine and may not serve as true differentiators unless they are from highly recognized individuals. So, ask everybody you work with to offer their specific, positive praise of you and your work and reach out to people you respect. Connect with them, and when the time is right, ask them to supply you with a testimonial of your work.

- *Establish an advisory board.* If well-known individuals will lend you their names, it will help you establish credibility within your target market. Just your association with other recognized experts will do wonders for establishing your credibility.

Standards of Service

These are the basic standards of service that are essential for any decent service professional to adhere to and that your clients will expect. The mistake that many service professionals make is thinking that these standards of service are all that are necessary to help them stand out from the crowd.

- *Quality of service.* Of course you should have a high quality of service! In fact, a potential client expects that you offer a high quality of service.

- *Methods and tools.* It's expected that you have the best methods and tools.
- *Responsiveness.* Your clients and customers expect you to be responsive. If you own an ambulance service, maybe responsiveness is paramount, but if you're a photographer, I expect you to respond to my calls and e-mails, but I don't expect you to come to my house on a whim at 3 A.M. on a Sunday to take a family portrait.
- *Credentials.* For most service professionals, clients don't care as much about credentials as you might think, unless, of course, you're in the medical, legal, or financial field; then credentials are expected and assumed. But you don't get a lot of brownie points for having a degree in acupuncture. If I'm going to come to you for acupuncture, I'll expect that you're credentialed, and if there is a plaque on the wall that displays your credentials, I'm satisfied. However, if you won the Nobel Peace Prize for your work as an acupuncturist, that would be a different story.
- *Client importance.* Your clients and customers expect to be considered important. It's essential to always make your clients feel important—more than important, in fact. You want to make your clients feel like the sun rises and shines just for them. It's essential that you do this to book yourself solid. It builds your credibility, but it should be a given.
- *Lowest price.* People don't generally buy on price (even though they say they do) and certainly not when it comes to their personal satisfaction, family, or their business, which I guess, is almost everything. Offering the lowest price is not necessarily going to help you establish credibility. In fact, many potential clients may be leery if your prices are significantly below market value.

Please do not assume that these standards of service will set you apart. They won't. They're what every savvy consumer will expect. However, there is something very special that will make you stand out from the crowd every day of the week.

Becoming and Establishing Yourself as a Category Authority

Although being a category authority and establishing yourself as one may, at first glance, appear to be the same thing, they're not. There is a distinction between the two. This isn't about faking it until you make it. Before you can establish yourself as a category authority you must *be* one. How do you do that? You truly become a category authority by learning everything you possibly can about the one thing you've decided you want to become known for.

If the thought of becoming and establishing yourself as a category authority immediately induces a sense of panic at the thought of all you'd have to learn and do, you're not alone. Or maybe you feel you already know enough to be an expert, but the thought of having to put yourself so boldly—and publicly—front and center of your target market makes you want to run home for Mom's homemade chicken soup.

For many of us, the leap into learning all we can about our field quickly becomes overwhelming, as often the first thing we learn is just how much we don't know. This is a good thing because you can't seek knowledge that you don't know you need, and yet, it may not feel very good at first.

For some, the idea of putting yourself out in front of the people you'd like to serve in a big, bold, public way, where you'll be subject to public scrutiny, can trigger a multitude of insecurities. You'll know your dark side has taken over when thoughts start racing round-and-round in your head like, "Who am I to call myself an expert? What do I know? I'm such a fraud. I don't know enough yet. Maybe I'll never learn enough to be an expert. I don't even know where to begin." Or worse yet, "What if I put myself out there and fall flat on my face? What if I look silly and embarrass myself? What if everyone hates me? What if I get made fun of or criticized?" Does this sound familiar? I'll bet it does. Again, you're not alone! It doesn't have to be that way. If your dark side is running rampant, lock it in a soundproof closet and give control back to the bold and brilliant you that you know you truly are, and keep reading.

Do I Have To?

If, now that you've avoided the dark side, some other side of you has taken over and is whining, "Do I have to?" the answer is a firm and resounding, "Yes! You do." Like it or not, becoming a category authority, an expert in your field, isn't optional if you want your business to be as successful as it can be. It's a must. Becoming and establishing yourself as a category authority will have such a powerful effect on the success of your business, and will be so incredibly rewarding, that it's well worth the effort and *perceived* risk (which means no real risk at all).

Becoming a category authority will:

- Create the credibility and trust necessary for potential clients to feel comfortable and confident about purchasing your services, products, and programs.
- Gain you the visibility you'll need to reach all of your target market.
- Allow you to get your message out to the world in a big way as it raises awareness of yourself and your business *within* your target market. The idea is to be the first to come to mind when someone needs the kind of services, products, and programs that you offer.
- Help you gain clients and increase sales more easily and effortlessly while also allowing you to earn higher fees. It will give you the edge you need to stand out from the crowd of others who offer similar services, products, and programs. Suddenly, you'll no longer be just one of the masses.
- Make it much easier to move and expand into new markets of your choosing.
- Increase your own confidence in your ability to provide the best possible services, products, and programs to those who most need and want them.

Luna Designs

In the Heart of South Beach

Bellydance Costumes &
Accessories

Exotic Decor

Jewelry Clothing

Gifts & CDs

Incense

Luna Designs

In the Heart of South Beach

438 Espanola Way
Miami Beach, FL 33139
Tel. 305-532-2588
luna@sobeluna.com
www.sobeluna.com

Where to Begin

First you have to identify what you'd like to become known for within your target market. If what you want to be known for is too broad or you try to become a category authority on too many topics, you'll overwhelm yourself and confuse your target market.

By identifying and focusing on the one thing you most want to become known for, you simplify and speed up the process, leaving no question in the minds of those in your target market about your area of expertise. This will allow you to create a synergy, not only among your services, products, and programs but among all the techniques you'll use to establish yourself as a category authority.

To powerfully establish yourself as a category authority, you need to saturate your target market using a variety of techniques that demonstrate your expertise on a single subject. To do that you must focus, focus, focus!

2.5.1 Written Exercise: Please answer the following questions:

1. In what areas are you currently an expert?
2. In what areas do you need to develop your expertise?
3. What promises can you make and deliver to your target market that will position you as an expert?
4. What promises would you like to make and deliver to your target market but don't yet feel comfortable with?
5. What do you need to do to become comfortable at making and delivering these promises?

2.5.2 Written Exercise: Keeping the answers from Written Exercise 2.5.1 in mind, if there was *one thing* you could be known for within your target market, what would it be?

> **2.5.3 Written Exercise:** What do you need to *learn* to become a category authority in the area you'd like to be known for?

> **2.5.4 Written Exercise:** List the ways in which you could learn the things you identified in Written Exercise 2.5.3.
>
> *Example:* Books, Internet research, training programs, apprenticing with a mentor who is already a category authority.

Even if you're already very knowledgeable about whatever it is you want to become known for, continuing to learn and staying up to date with the latest information in your field is not only a good idea but required to remain booked solid. I recommend that you read at least one book a month, if not more, on your chosen subject, which will increase your knowledge, challenge you to see a different perspective, or spark new ideas and thoughts, all of which will enhance the value you provide to your clients.

> **2.5.5 Written Exercise:** Research and list five books that meet the above criteria.

> **2.5.6 Booked Solid Action Step:** Buy these five books.

Making the Mental Shift

We've discussed what you need to have and do to be credible, and by now you understand the importance of becoming and establishing yourself as a category authority. I hope it's clear that you must actually *be* an expert. You might think the logical next step would be to implement a plan to establish yourself as a category authority within your target market, but it's not. There's a critical mental shift that must take place first.

All of the Book Yourself Solid marketing strategies that you're going to learn in Module Three will put you out in front of your target market in such a big way that you will establish yourself as a category authority. First consider what you need to learn and what you need to do in order to establish your expertise so when the time comes to implement the Book Yourself Solid 7 Core Self-Promotion Strategies, you will *be* an expert. You will make the crucial mental shift of thinking of yourself as an expert. If *you* don't believe it, you'll have a hard time convincing anyone else of it.

> *Begin to think of and refer to yourself as a category authority—an expert in your field.*

When the time comes to establish yourself as a category authority within your target market, you'll be comfortable with, and confident of, your expertise. If you already consider yourself an expert, then by all means begin including that in your current marketing materials.

Just remember—when communicating with your potential clients, be clear about what you know and clear about what you don't. People who are credible don't actually know everything, and they are just as comfortable saying that they don't know something as they are saying that they do.

There is one other very powerful mental/emotional factor that has a profound impact on your efforts to establish yourself as a category authority, one that may surprise you. I urge you not to discount or underestimate it.

The Power of Likeability

Now that you know what you need to do to become and establish yourself as a category authority, we're going to look at an even more important factor to consider: Do your potential clients like you? Do they perceive you as likeable? And I mean *really* likeable.

The fact is that if they don't, none of the rest of your efforts to establish yourself as a category authority will matter. That's a pretty bold statement, and it may come as a surprise to you, but bear with me as I shine some light on the subject, with the help of Tim Sanders and a few concepts from his book, *The Likeability Factor: How to Boost Your L-Factor and Achieve Your Life's Dreams.*

When you get right down to it, Sanders points out, "Life is a series of popularity contests." We don't want to admit it, we don't want to believe it, we've been told it ain't necessarily so, but ultimately, if you're well-liked, if your likeability factor is high, you're more likely to be chosen and to get booked solid.

Mark McCormack, the founder of International Management Group (IMG), the most powerful sports management and marketing company, agrees: "All things being equal, people will do business with a friend; all things being unequal, people will still do business with a friend." If a potential client perceives you as the most credible and likeable, you're probably the one they'll hire. And even if all things are *not* equal, even if you aren't the candidate with the most experience or expertise, if your potential client likes you, it's your likeability that will win the day and the client.

Sanders also reveals that "to make choices, we go through a three-step process. First, we *listen* to something out of a field of opportunities. Then we either do or do not *believe* what we've heard. Finally, we put a *value* on what we've heard." Then we make our choice.

With so many demands on our attention these days, we have to filter and carefully select what we give our attention to. This is why becoming and establishing yourself as a category authority is so important. Your target market and your potential clients need a reason to deem your message important enough to sit up and pay attention, to *listen* to it. If you're likeable, they're much more likely to do so and to remember what they've heard.

Once you've got their attention, they're listening, but will they *believe* what they're hearing? This is where your credibility comes into play. With so many advertising messages coming at us from every direction each day—through spam e-mail, radio and TV commercials, and infomercials, to name a few—we've become highly skeptical of much of what we hear. If you're credible, you're much more likely to be believed.

But wait, that's not the only factor that comes into play when someone is determining whether to believe you. Again, your likeability is a critical factor in establishing trust. Think about it for a moment. You're much more likely to trust, and to *believe,* someone you like. Sanders says, "When people like the source of a message, they tend to trust the message or, at least, try to find a way to believe it."

Let's suppose that you've made it through the first two steps of this process. Your potential client has listened to you and believes you. Now she must determine the value of you and your message. Consider this example:

Susan owns a spa and is interviewing two massage therapists. They both have relatively equal qualifications: They have been practicing for 12 years, are certified in Shiatsu, deep tissue, sports, Swedish, and relaxation massage, and expect to be paid around $100 per hour.

The first massage therapist walks into the interview 10 minutes late, frowning and obviously agitated. She then launches into a litany of complaints about her day to explain her delayed arrival. This candidate leaves Susan feeling on edge and irritated. Susan realizes very quickly that her clients and staff are likely to have a similar negative reaction to this massage therapist's demeanor.

The second massage therapist is waiting patiently for her interview when Susan finishes with the first. She beams a radiant smile at Susan as she enters the office. Her upbeat temperament has a profound and immediate effect on Susan, and she feels herself relax as she smiles back. She already knows that her clients and staff will love her.

As this scenario demonstrates, your likeability factor can have an enormous impact on your perceived value. Develop your credibility, establish yourself as an expert, strive to be your best, most likeable self, and you'll quickly become the best and most obvious choice for your potential clients.

6

The Book Yourself Solid Sales Cycle Process

It is a mistake to look too far ahead. Only one link in the chain of destiny can be handled at a time.

—Sir Winston Churchill

Building Relationships of Trust

All sales start with a simple conversation. It may be a conversation between you and a potential client or customer, between one of your clients and a potential referral, or between one of your colleagues and a potential referral. An effective sales cycle is based on turning these simple conversations into relationships of trust with your potential clients over time. We know that people buy from those they like and trust. This is never truer than for the professional service provider.

If you don't have trust, then it doesn't matter how well you've planned, what you're offering, or whether you've created a wide variety of buying options to meet varying budgets. If a potential client doesn't trust you, nothing else matters. They aren't going to buy from you—period. If you think about it, this may be one of the main reasons you say you hate marketing and selling. You may be trying to market and sell to people with whom you have not yet built trust.

What are your potential clients thinking?

- Do they really believe you can deliver what you say you can?
- Do they trust you to hold their personal information confidential?
- Do they like the people who work for you?
- Do they feel safe with you?
- Do they believe hiring you will give them a significant return on their investment?

If you want a perpetual stream of inspiring and life-fulfilling ideal clients clamoring for your services and products, then just remember—all sales start with a simple conversation and are executed when a need is met and trust is assured.

Turn Strangers into Friends and Friends into Clients

Seth Godin, author of *Permission Marketing*, implores us to stop interrupting people with our marketing messages and instead turn strangers into friends by adding value and friends into customers by getting permission from them to offer our products and services. In its most effective form, the Book Yourself Solid Sales Cycle not only turns strangers into friends and friends into potential clients but potential clients into current clients and past clients into current clients.

In order to design a sales cycle for your business, you must first understand how you're going to lead people into your sales cycle. Then we can actually build out a sales cycle process that will attract more clients than you can handle and do so with the utmost integrity.

The Book Yourself Solid Six Keys to Creating Connection: Who, What, Where, When, Why, and How

The Book Yourself Solid Sales Cycle works when you know:

1. *Who* your target clients or customers are.
2. *What* they are looking for.
3. *Where* they look for you.
4. *When* they look for you.
5. *Why* they should choose you.
6. *How* you want them to engage with you.

Know your responses to these six keys and you will ensure that the offers you are making in your sales cycle process are right on target.

Key #1: Who Is Your Target Client or Customer?

We've covered in depth how to choose a target market, but I'm going to re-iterate it here because of its importance. You need to choose whom you'd like to bring into your cycle. The more specific you are the better; choose one person (or organization) within your target market to focus on.

Identifying and gearing your marketing to a specific individual (or organization) allows you to make the important emotional connection that is the first step in developing a relationship with your potential client. When you have made the effort to speak and write directly to your ideal client, he'll feel it. He will feel as though you truly know and understand his needs and desires—because you will. That task alone will go a long way toward building the trust you desire with the clients you seek.

If you're not super clear on whom specifically you're targeting, whom you want to reach out to and attract, it's going to be hard to develop a sales cycle that works because you'll be chasing after every potential opportunity and you won't be making a strong connection with anyone.

2.6.1 Written Exercise: *Who* is your target client/customer? Describe what he or she is like. Get really creative with this one. List as many specific details as you can.

Example: My friend and colleague Lorrie Morgan Ferrero, a well-known copywriter and the owner of www.Red-Hot-Copy.com, describes her target customer like this: "Nikki Stanton, a 37-year-old divorced entrepreneur with a web conferencing business. She's Internet and business savvy. Invests most of her profit back into the business. Lives in San Diego in a gated community with her 10-year-old daughter, Madison. She's involved in her daughter's school and drives her to dance classes. Has a home office making approximately $117,000 a year. Jogs three times a week in the neighborhood. She loves to find bargains on designer clothes and dreams of visiting Italy with her daughter someday."

Your turn. Describe whom you'd like to attract into your sales cycle.

Key #2: What Are They Looking For?

You've got to understand what your ideal clients or customers are looking for. It's very important to be clear on your answers because if you don't know what your potential clients are looking for, you won't know what kind of offers to make to them in your sales cycle. We usually make offers that *we* think are relevant. It's time to put your target market first and work to truly understand what they are looking for. Then you can decide what you're going to offer them that will meet their needs.

2.6.2 Written Exercise: *What* are your potential clients looking for?

Examples: They want to book themselves solid so they have financial freedom. They want to get organized so they can make more sales. They want to develop multiple streams of passive revenue so they don't have to trade time for money. They want to deepen their relationship with their partner so they don't feel alone in the world. Remember, always ask yourself the *so-that* question. They want to book themselves solid *so that* they can have financial freedom.

Key #3: When Do They Look for You?

When do the people (or organizations) in your target market look for the services you offer? What needs to happen in their personal life or work life for them to purchase the kind of service that you offer? How high do the stakes need to be before they decide to purchase the service you're offering? They may be interested in what you do, and your offerings may resonate with them, but they might not need you at the moment they find you.

This is why the Book Yourself Solid Sales Cycle is so important. You'll want to make it easy for them to step into your environment and move closer and closer to your core offerings over time. When their stakes rise, they'll reach out to you and ask for you. But you've got to keep the conversation going.

> **2.6.3 Written Exercise:** Describe the situations that are likely to drive potential clients to seek your services, products, and programs. *When* do they look for you?
>
> *Examples:* They've lost their job. They're starting their own business. They're so disorganized that they're losing business. They are experiencing extreme discord in their relationship. They've just had a baby and can't seem to lose their baby weight.

Key #4: Where Do They Look for You?

Do you know where your target market looks for you? Do they search online? Do they read magazines? Do they call their friends for referrals for the kind of service that you're providing? What other types of business professionals do they trust to get their referrals from? If you don't know, survey your current clients. This should always be one of the first questions you ask a new client: "How did you come to find me?" If you don't have any clients of your own yet, ask a colleague how her clients find her.

> **2.6.4 Written Exercise:** *Where* do your ideal clients look for you?

Key #5: Why You?

That's a big question. Why are they going to choose you? Are you a credible authority in your field? What makes you the best choice for them? What is unique about you or the solutions you offer?

For this exercise, it's crucial that you set your modesty aside and express yourself clearly and with confidence—no wishy-washy answers to these questions. Think back to the last time you went in search of expert help. When you first spoke to the service provider to inquire about his services, his expertise, and whether he could help you, the *last* thing you wanted to hear was, "Well, I kinda know what I'm doing. I might be able to help you. I'll give it a shot."

> *While it may feel uncomfortable at first, you've got to get comfortable saying, "The best thing for you is me!"*

Granted, saying you are the best may be a bit too bold for you, but at the least you've got to be able to say, "You've come to the perfect person. Yes, absolutely, I *can* help you. I'm an expert at what I do and this is how I can help."

Bragging is about comparing yourself to others and proclaiming your superiority. Declaring your strengths, your skills, your expertise, and your ability to help is not bragging. It's what your potential clients expect, want, and need to hear from you.

2.6.5 Written Exercise: *Why* should your potential clients choose you? (Don't you dare skip this one! Be bold! Express yourself fully. Remember, this is not the time for modesty.)

Key #6: How Do You Want Them to Engage with You?

Once potential clients have learned about your services, how would you like them to interact or engage with you? Do you want them to call your office? Do you want them to sign up for your newsletter on your web site? What is it that you want potential clients to *do*?

Naturally, we'd love for them to immediately purchase our highest-priced product, program, or service, but this is rare. Most of your potential clients need to get to know you and trust you over time. They need to be eased gradually toward what they may perceive to be your high-risk offerings. It's often said that, on average, you will need to connect with a potential client seven times before they'll purchase from you. Not always, but if you understand this principle you will be on the road to booking yourself solid a lot faster than if you try to engage in one-step selling. "Hi, I'm a consultant, wanna hire me today?" isn't going to be effective. That's definitely not the Book Yourself Solid way. Maybe we should call one-step selling one-*stop* selling because that's what it'll do—stop your sales process dead in its tracks.

2.6.6 Written Exercise: *How* do you want your potential clients to interact or engage with you? (Note: Establishing a line of communication is the first step in developing a relationship of trust.)

Clearly defining these six keys will help you to determine what you want to offer your potential clients in each stage of your sales cycle and will help you craft the most effective sales cycle possible. (I'll be stepping you through designing your sales cycle shortly.) Defining these six keys will also help you tremendously when implementing the Book Yourself Solid 7 Core Self-Promotion Strategies.

The Book Yourself Solid Always-Have-Something-to-Invite-People-to Offer

This strategy is simply the most effective marketing strategy on the planet for the professional service provider. You'll want to consider your own always-have-something-to-invite-people-to offer as you design your Book

Yourself Solid Sales Cycle. This is what you'll direct potential clients to when you use the Book Yourself Solid 7 Core Self-Promotion Strategies revealed in Module Three.

Your services have a high barrier for entry. To potential new clients, your services are intangible and expensive—whether you think they are or not—especially to those who have not used the kind of services that you offer or who have not had good results with their previous service providers. People usually hate to be sold, but they love to receive invitations. Don't you? What if I could help you eliminate your need to sell with this one solution? Would that be exciting to you? I bet it would. By my second year in business, this one strategy literally doubled my income.

The Book Yourself Solid Sales Cycle begins by making no-barrier-to-entry offers to potential clients. A no-barrier-to-entry offer is one that has no risk whatsoever for a potential client so that he can *sample* your services. I'm not talking about offering free services, which is a common practice for many professional service providers. I take this concept much farther with much more success.

You will use the Book Yourself Solid 7 Core Self-Promotion Strategies, including networking, Web, direct outreach, referral, writing, speaking, and keep-in-touch, to create awareness for the solutions you offer. However, rather than attempting to *sell* a client, you will simply offer him an invitation that has no barrier for entry.

We've learned that "who knows *what* you know" is important when attempting to book yourself solid. Do you realize how many more clients you could be serving if they just knew what you had to offer? The best way to inform them is to have at least one compelling offer that has no barrier for entry.

One of mine is a complimentary teleseminar (very large conference call) that I've named the Think Big Revolution. I offer it on a weekly basis, and it's designed to help people think bigger about who they are and what they offer the world. Sometimes I discuss a topic that is specifically related to getting more clients, and other times I discuss different principles and strategies that will help the callers be more successful in business and in life.

Note that the membership is free. If I meet someone who I think will benefit from membership, I invite him to join. I'd like to invite you. I bet you'll love it. You get an opportunity to participate in something that should add great value to your life and test me out at the same time. And for me it's fantastic because I don't have to *sell* anything. I can offer really great value to the lives of potential clients and customers at no risk to them. And then they have the opportunity to ask me for more business help if they are so inclined.

There are many ways you can set up this kind of always-have-something-to-invite-people-to self-promotion strategy. You are limited only by the scope of your imagination. If ideas for your own always-have-something-to-invite-people-to offer are just not springing to life for you right now, don't fret. I'm going to give you plenty of specific ideas and ways of brainstorming your own in Module Three.

To accept my invitation to join the Think Big Revolution, go to www.ThinkBigRevolution.com and sign up there. See how easy that was? No selling; just a generous invitation.

This strategy works! Of the 93 percent of my clients who successfully book themselves solid, all of them use it in one form or another.

There is another added benefit of this kind of always-have-something-to-invite-people-to offer. It can serve as one of the most effective ways of establishing your personal brand. Notice how the Think Big Revolution is an extension of my *why I do it* statement. Once you come to a Think Big Revolution weekly member meeting, you'll immediately see that I want to help you think bigger about who you are and what you offer the world. And if you're someone who wants to think bigger about who you are and what you offer the world, then you'll know you're in the right place, not just intellectually, but in your soul as well. Your always-have-something-to-invite-people-to offer is the perfect way to integrate and align your *who and do what* statement (whom you help and what you help them do) and your *why you do it* statement (the philosophical reason that you do what you do).

Consider another example: I worked with a man who is a personal trainer and a healthy-eating chef. When he came to me, he was facing two challenges that he needed my help with. He was not living up to his full income potential due to working with clients only on a one-on-one basis, and he hadn't created a relentless demand for his services. Both of these concerns caused him to be anxious over what his future held.

First I asked him to look at how we could adapt his services from just offering one-on-one training, to group programs. Then we created his always-have-something-to-invite-people-to offer: the *Fitness Fiesta for Foodies*. One Sunday evening a month, he would hold a party where he would teach his guests how to prepare healthful meals that help them stay fit. There were two requirements for attendance, however. He would put that month's menu on his web site and each guest was required to bring one item off the menu. Each guest was also asked to bring someone new to the event, thus creating a new audience for his work. He barely had to market himself. It was magical. People loved it and they loved him for doing it. And they joined his programs because of it.

A financial planner could do something similar either on the phone or in person. Even a simple Q&A about building wealth would do the trick. Are you beginning to get your own ideas on how this could work for you?

The value you add in your offer meets the needs and desires of the people you serve. This no-barrier-for-entry offer is an essential component of the Book Yourself Solid Sales Cycle. Then as you continue to build trust over time by offering additional value and creating awareness for the services you provide, you'll attract potential clients deeper into the sales cycle, moving them closer to your core offerings.

You'll notice that the two always-have-something-to-invite-people-to examples I offered are done in a group format. There are three important reasons for this:

1. You'll leverage your time so you're connecting with as many potential clients as possible in the shortest amount of time.
2. You'll leverage the power of communities. When you bring people together, they create far more energy and excitement than you can

on your own. Your guests will also see other people interested in what you have to offer, and that's the best way to build credibility.

3. You'll be viewed as a really cool person. Seriously, if you're known in your marketplace as someone who brings people together, that will help you build your reputation and increase your likeability.

Please give away so much value that you think you've given too much and then give more. I had a friend in college who, when he ordered his hero sandwiches, would say, "Put so much mayonnaise on it that you think you've ruined it, and then put more." Gross, I know (I believe that he has since stopped eating his sandwiches that way and his arteries are thanking him), but adding value is not a dissimilar experience. Remember, your potential clients must know *what* you know. They must really like you and believe that you have the solutions to their very personal, specific, and urgent problems. The single best way to do that is to invite them to experience what it's like to be around you and the people you serve.

The Book Yourself Solid Sales Cycle Process

The sales cycle works in a way that allows buyers to enter at any point in the process, depending on their situation. A client hires you when the circumstances in his or her life or work match the offers that you make. If you're a mortgage specialist, I may not need your services right now. But perhaps, six months from now, I stumble upon a FOR SALE sign in the front yard of my dream home. You can bet that I'll not only want your services, I'll need them immediately. Do you see how the stakes have changed? Chances are that if you haven't built trust with me over the last six months by offering great value along the way (without expecting anything in return, mind you), it's unlikely you'll cross my mind when I look to secure a mortgage for my dream house.

The Book Yourself Solid Sales Cycle is a sequence of phases that a client moves through when deciding whether to buy your services or products. The following example will give you a framework for the process. Your sales cycle may include 3, 10, or even 15 stages, depending on your particular business and the different services and products you offer. I'm going to teach you the principles that govern an effective sales cycle so that you can craft one that serves your particular business and meets the individual needs and tastes of your clients and customers.

I will explain each stage and give you a real example from my business to help you visualize exactly how each stage works. I'm going to also ask you to write out your objective for each stage and how you're going to achieve your objective. This way, by the end of the chapter you'll have completed your very own Book Yourself Solid Sales Cycle. I'll do my best to make it as easy as possible to absorb and implement the information. If you do get a bit overwhelmed, please stay with it. This is an important part of the Book Yourself Solid system, and understanding the principles behind these techniques will ensure that you're well on your way to being booked solid.

As you work through this process, remember you are simply having a conversation with someone. You are making a connection that will build trust so that you will then be able to share your services with another person. How cool is that?

Book Yourself Solid Sales Cycle—Stage One

To book yourself solid, you must perform daily tasks that will keep your name in front of potential clients. In stage one your objective is to create awareness for the services, products, and programs you offer through the Book Yourself Solid 7 Core Self-Promotion Strategies (coming in more detail in Module Three of this book). You will have your choice of:

1. The Book Yourself Solid Networking Strategy.
2. The Book Yourself Solid Direct Outreach Strategy.
3. The Book Yourself Solid Referral Strategy.
4. The Book Yourself Solid Web Strategy.
5. The Book Yourself Solid Speaking and Demonstrating Strategy.

6. The Book Yourself Solid Writing Strategy.

7. The Book Yourself Solid Keep-in-Touch Strategy.

Your objective for stage one of the Book Yourself Solid Sales Cycle should be simple and measurable, like driving prospective clients to your web site. Or maybe you want them to call your office directly. It's up to you. But once you've chosen an objective, you'll choose the strategies you would like to use to achieve it.

The Book Yourself Solid Sales Cycle is most effective when used in conjunction with a keep-in-touch plan. The size of your network, and especially the number of potential clients in your network, is directly proportional to how booked solid you are. I strongly suggest working diligently on building up your database—or your list, as it's called in the Internet marketing world. Your list is made up of people who have given you permission to communicate with them on an ongoing basis. They are made up of your potential, current, and past clients, as well as your colleagues and referral sources. Building a large list and having permission to communicate with them will make it easy to secure new clients whenever you need to. All you have to do is send out a newsletter or e-newsletter, make a compelling offer, and *voilà!*—you'll have new ideal clients. I don't mean to sound glib, but you'll see just how easy it is once you build trust with a large group of raving fans who have given you permission to add value to their lives and make offers to them at the same time.

Michael's Stage One Example   My stage one objective is to drive potential clients to my web site. I use the Book Yourself Solid Web Strategy, the Book Yourself Solid Speaking and Demonstrating Strategy, and the Book Yourself Solid Writing Strategy. (You'll learn these strategies in Chapters 12, 13, and 14, respectively.)

2.6.7 Written Exercise: Book Yourself Solid Sales Cycle Stage One:

- What is your objective in stage one of the sales cycle?
- How are you going to achieve it?

Book Yourself Solid Sales Cycle—Stage Two

In this stage you will demonstrate your knowledge, solutions, and sincere desire to provide value to your target market free of charge, with no barrier to entry and at no risk to them. The benefits include increased trust— they will feel as though they know you somewhat better.

In order to familiarize your prospective clients with your services, you need to offer them solutions, opportunities, and relevant information in exchange for their contact information and permission to continue communicating with them over time. What does that communication look like? You may provide a special report or white paper that addresses their urgent needs and compelling desires. You might give a discount coupon for your initial session. It could be your always-have-something-to-invite-people-to offer, like my Think Big Revolution. No matter what you select, it should be something that speaks not only to their needs but also to how you want to be known.

Michael's Stage Two Example   My stage two objective is to encourage my web site visitors to enter their name, e-mail address, and location in exchange for a free chapter from this book along with a high-quality 60-minute audio recording in which I expand on the concepts, principles, and strategies.

2.6.8 Written Exercise: Book Yourself Solid Sales Cycle Stage Two:

- What is your objective in stage two of the cycle?
- How are you going to achieve it?

Book Yourself Solid Sales Cycle—Stage Three

Now that you've started building trust between you and your potential clients, you're going to work on developing and enhancing that trust and cultivating the relationship.

In stage three of the sales cycle your objective is twofold: to continue to add value by helping your potential clients incorporate the information that you gave them in stage two of the cycle and to make a sale. If you gave them a minicourse, you should follow up with automated e-mails. Or if you invited them to your always-have-something-to-invite-people-to event, you'll tell them more about it, make sure they know how to take advantage of it, and of course, what the benefits of participating in it will be. You should also offer them something that will surprise them. It could be a complimentary pass to a workshop you're doing or a personal note on your stationery or branded postcard with a list of books on your area of expertise that you know will speak to their urgent needs. Remember, the value you add doesn't have to be all about you. If you recommend a resource to your potential clients, they will very likely associate the value they received from that resource with you.

As I mentioned, this is the first stage of the sales cycle where you also offer your potential clients a service or product that will cost them money: an in-person seminar or intake session. It might be one of your information products: e-book, published book, CD, DVD, workbook, manual, guidebook, or teleseminar. (I teach you how to create these kinds of information products in Chapter 7.) When you send your follow-up e-mails, you will let your potential clients know of the opportunities you have for them that speak directly to their urgent needs and compelling desires, and you'll continue to add value without expecting anything in return.

What's important to understand is that the monetized offer you are making does not have a very high barrier to entry. You're not going to rush out of the gate and surprise potential clients with your highest-priced offer, just as you wouldn't propose marriage on a first date, no matter how smitten you are. You want to offer them something that they are ready for, and if they're ready for more at that moment, they'll ask for it. You'll always let potential clients know how to view the page on your web site that lists your various services, just in case they are ready to walk down the aisle.

Michael's Stage Three Example   My stage three objective is to give those who previously opted in for the free chapter and 60-minute audio the incentive to purchase this book from Amazon.com. (You don't have to have a published book to do this. You can offer an intake session, needs assessment, e-book, CD, class, or any other low-barrier-for-entry offer.)

2.6.9 Written Exercise: Book Yourself Solid Sales Cycle Stage Three:

- What is your objective in stage three of the cycle?
- How are you going to achieve it?

Book Yourself Solid Sales Cycle—Stage Four

Your focus now is to help your potential clients move to the next level of your sales cycle. Let's say a potential client bought your low-barrier-for-entry product or service or has even become a client, thanks to your efforts in stage three of the sales cycle. Now is the time to over-deliver on the product or service he purchased. What does that mean? Here's an example: Your client has recently purchased your e-book, and you notice that you have a workshop or presentation scheduled on the very same topic. To over-deliver, you could send the customer an e-mail inviting him to the workshop or, if he can't attend, send him a copy of the notes after the event. What a great way to give more than the potential client expected to receive.

When he has received great value from that service or product, you then offer your next level of product or service, something that requires more of an investment than the previous product or service he purchased. Notice how this client is moving closer and closer to your core offerings and your higher-priced offerings. This is usually the case but only after you've increased the client's trust factor and proven that your solutions work and that you deliver on the promises that you make.

If the potential client does not engage in one of your stage three offerings right away, don't despair. Just remember that you are building relationships of trust that will grow and, you hope, last a lifetime. When the time is right, a potential client will become a current client.

Michael's Stage Four Example   My stage four objective is to enroll people in my live Book Yourself Solid seminars throughout the United States and Canada, the same people who have already visited my web site, opted in for a free chapter and audio recording, and purchased my book.

I believe that when people have read my book, thoughtfully done the exercises, and taken the Booked Solid Action Steps necessary, they will be well on their way to getting booked solid. They will also be confident that what I have to offer them is valid and valuable and that I can serve their most relevant, personal, and immediate needs and desires. However, they may also want the opportunity to work through the concepts, principles, and strategies in the book with me, my team, and other inspired service professionals live and in person for a number of reasons: opportunity for more personal coaching and attention, higher levels of accountability, networking opportunities, or maybe they want to bathe in the Book Yourself Solid fountain of inspiration.

The point is, I don't want to introduce them to the live events until they've had the opportunity to read the book. I want them to be excited about meeting me and my team and know that we can serve them before they come to one of the live events. That one factor, knowing that we can serve them, will give our participants better results, and that's our goal—to help our clients get the results they want. Isn't that your goal? Furthermore, I know from past experience that it will also increase attendance at the events. Will there be people at the events who have not yet read the book? Sure, but more people will enroll in the events after they have read the book. Your goal throughout the sales cycle is to help people move closer and closer to your core offerings by ensuring that they are getting the results they need at each stage of the cycle.

Each stage of this cycle applies to you regardless of whether you're holding live events for 400 people or you have a small graphic design firm. To do the following exercise, you are going to simply replace my offering of a live event with the appropriate offer for you and your clients. Remember, your sales cycle will have as many stages as is appropriate for you and your business right now. It will evolve as your business evolves.

2.6.10 Written Exercise: Book Yourself Solid Sales Cycle Stage Four:

- What is your objective in stage four of the cycle?
- How are you going to achieve it?

Book Yourself Solid Sales Cycle—Stage Five

Your objective in stage five is similar to the previous one: to help potential clients move to the next level of your sales cycle by offering them a higher-level product or service. What's important to understand about this process is that not every person or organization who enters into your sales cycle will move all the way through it, and the time that each potential client takes to do so will be different as well.

Michael's Stage Five Example My stage five objective is to enroll ideal clients into my Book Yourself Solid Intensive Coaching Programs. Again, there are many people who join one of the programs without attending a live event, or right after they read my book, or even before they do, simply because they were referred to me by a person they trust. But you can't count on that. You'll have better success if you lay out a plan for how you introduce people to your offerings.

The Book Yourself Solid Intensive Coaching Programs require more of a time commitment as well as financial investment than do the live events. That's why it's very important to me that those who join these programs know that it is the right place for them to continue their business development and trust that my team and I will over-deliver on our promises. I imagine you would want the same thing. After people attend a live event, which is my stage four offering, they should believe this deeply. This is why the Book Yourself Solid Sales Cycle is so effective. You're building trust with people over time, trust that is proportionate to the size of the offer you're making to them.

As a professional service provider you don't want to try to convince people that what you're offering is right for them. You want to provide value upon value until they know that your services are right for them. They will get better results that way and be more satisfied with your services, a factor that is way too important to forget about.

2.6.11 Written Exercise: Book Yourself Solid Sales Cycle Stage Five:

- What is your objective in stage five of the cycle?
- How are you going to achieve it?

Use the Book Yourself Solid Sales Cycle to Unconditionally Serve Your Clients

You can have as many stages to your sales cycle as you need in order to build trust with potential clients for the kinds of offers you make. Just thinking about your sales cycle will help you clarify and expand your offerings. Gone are the days when you can simply have one offering and be guaranteed to book yourself solid. The marketplace is too competitive and diverse. Every day another inspired professional stakes a claim and joins the ranks of free agents around the world. More and more people are feeling the call to stand in the service of others.

Expanding your offerings in order to create a Book Yourself Solid Sales Cycle may just enhance your business model—the mechanism by which you generate revenue—from only one offering with one stream of revenue to multiple offerings with multiple streams of revenue.

The Book Yourself Solid Sales Cycle is not just about getting new clients to hire you. It is designed to unconditionally serve your current clients as well. It is much harder to sell your services, products, and programs to a new client than to those who have already received value from you as a client or customer. The most successful businesses, both large and small, know this. It's one of the reasons Amazon.com is so successful. Once you've become a customer, they know you, they know what you need, what you read, and they work to continue to serve you. The typical client-snagging mentality suggests that you make a sale and move on. The Book Yourself Solid way requires that you make a sale and ask, "How can I over-deliver and continue to serve this person or organization?" This is not a small thing.

Now it's your turn to develop your own unique sales cycle. Don't limit yourself to just the few examples I've already touched on. There are a multitude of ways to build trust with your potential clients and to ease them toward purchasing your higher price point offerings. Use your imagination and creativity to tailor your sales cycle to what works best, feels most natural, and resonates most with you.

7

The Power of Information Products

Know where to find the information and how to use it—that's the secret of success.

—Albert Einstein

Brand-Building Products and Easy-to-Follow Programs

Much of the information in this chapter comes from a coaching program that I co-created with my good friend and business partner, Mitch Meyerson, called *The Product Factory: 90 Days to a Signature Product or Program* (www.90DayProduct.com).

Nothing helps to build your credibility like products and programs designed to serve your target market's very specific urgent needs and compelling desires. People love to buy packaged learning and experiences. It's very easy for them to understand what they are buying when they buy a program or a product from you. Your service may not be as easily defined and may have a very high barrier for entry. As you continue to develop and enhance your Book Yourself Solid Sales Cycle, you will want to produce products and programs that will fully round out the many stages of your sales cycle.

I'm sure your bookshelves are lined with products and programs that you've purchased from other service professionals over the years. In fact, you're reading one now. How would you like to create your own self-expression product or program? I use the phrase *self-expression* because the kind of programs and products that I'm referring to gives you an opportunity to express yourself to the world and serve your target market at the same time. That's the beauty of being a service professional.

> *You are in the business of serving other people as you stand in the service of your destiny and express yourself through your work.*

I just love the opportunity offered through information product creation because you can follow a simple step-by-step system that leads you to the production of the kind of revenue and satisfaction that comes from bold self-expression. Let's take a quick look at the other red-hot benefits that you get from producing information products:

- Products create opportunities for multiple streams of passive or leveraged income. They can be in retail stores or online, at your web site and the web sites of your affiliates, 24×7×365, with worldwide availability. I consistently get orders for my products from people all over the world who saw them on one of my web sites or one of my affiliates' web sites.
- Having a product enhances your credibility with your prospects, your peers, meeting planners, and the media because it establishes you as an expert in your field and sets you apart from your competitors.
- Products can help you land more clients because they speed up the sales cycle. Since your services have a high barrier for entry, your potential clients may need to jump a few high hurdles to convince themselves they need to hire you. Having a product to offer based on your services gives potential clients the opportunity to test you out without having to take a big risk. Then if they connect with you and are well served by your product, they will upgrade from the lower-priced product to the higher-priced service.

- If you use public speaking as one of your marketing strategies, having a product at the back of the room when you speak gives you credibility, and you also have a relatively low-cost way to introduce prospects into your business and generate ancillary revenue at the same time.
- Products leverage your time. One of the biggest problems service professionals face is the paradigm of trading time for money. If all you ever do is trade your time for money, your revenues are limited by how much you charge per hour. For example, if you speak in front of 100 of your prospects and you're able to sell a couple dozen of your information products at $50 each, then you've just increased your hourly rate from $100 to over $1,000 an hour. Again, remember, many more people are willing and able to buy an information product than they are willing and able to hire you for your higher-priced service.

One of the first information products I developed and sold was a three-CD audio program on how to get more clients. I produced a results-oriented product for the members of my target market that positioned me as an expert in my field. It did my marketing for me. I no longer had to talk about what I could do to help. I was able to demonstrate my expertise.

Start with the End in Mind

You may be in the beginning phase of building your business and just be setting out on the course to book yourself solid, but as Dr. Stephen Covey (*The 7 Habits of Highly Successful People*) says, "Start with the end in mind." If you want to seriously build a long-lasting career as a service professional, you'll want to start thinking just as seriously about creating information products.

Don't let the idea of creating products intimidate you; you can start where you are and then the sky's the limit. For example, you can:

- Publish a free-tips book.
- Write an e-book.

- Produce an audio CD.
- Write an article.
- Write a workbook.
- Compile and publish a glossary of inspirational quotes.

Here are a few thoughts on your first self-expression product:

- Keep it simple.
- Don't overwork it or feel that it needs to be perfect.
- Don't worry about being wildly original.
- Tips, guides, or resource manuals are great formats.
- Continually strive to add value to your clients' lives in any way you can.

When considering how to create an information product, start by examining the different possibilities and ask yourself, "How can I leverage my existing knowledge and experience to create a quality product that I can produce and launch in the shortest amount of time possible?"

Be sure you don't overlook any content you may already have created. If you've written an article, you have content that you can leverage into multiple formats. You can quickly and easily turn your article into an e-course, use it as the foundation for an e-book, print book, or program, or present it as an introductory presentation or teleclass. A single article can be leveraged into any or all of these formats, making it possible to create an entire sales cycle from a single source of content.

Define Your Product or Program

Choose the one product idea that you're most passionate or excited about right now—and most important, one that is in line with your current business needs. If you're starting out and need to build your database, you'll need to create a *lead-generating* product first, a product that you give away to create connection with a potential client. You will then leverage that free lead-generating information product into other monetized information products over time. If you already have a lead-generating product and you're ready to produce higher-priced information products like an audio program or a book, then go for it!

As you define your product, you will need to consider not only the type of product you will create but to whom you're selling it, the promises it makes, the benefits and solutions it offers, the look and feel you want your product to convey, and the ways in which you can leverage the content.

2.7.1 Written Exercise: For now, keep it simple. Just get your ideas out of your head and onto paper.

1. What type of product or program would you most like to create? What would you be most passionate about creating and offering to your target market?
2. To whom would you be offering this product? (Refer to target market.)
3. What benefits will your target market experience as a result of your product?
4. How do you want your product to look and feel? What image and/or emotion do you want it to convey?
5. How might you leverage the same content into a variety of different formats and price points for your sales cycle?

Assess the Need

It's important to be clear about your intentions for your product or program, and it's critical that your product or program meet the needs of your target market. No matter how much you might love to create something, if your target market doesn't need it you'll be defeating your purpose.

2.7.2 Written Exercise: Answer the following questions:

- Why does your target market need your particular product now?
- What does your product need to deliver in order to meet your customer's need?
- What about your product, if anything, will be different from similar products on the market?
- *Bonus:* How can you over-deliver on your promises by adding unexpected value to make your product remarkable?

If you're unsure of your target market's need for a particular type of product or program, doing market research will help you ensure you're creating something your target market will find valuable. Survey friends, clients, and groups, such as online discussion groups or local organizations. Use online tools such as Google.com, Overture.com, and Clickbank.com to identify and assess competitive products and programs.

The Five Steps to Developing Your Content

These five simple steps to developing your content are discussed in the following subsections.

Step 1: Choose the role you are playing.

Step 2: Choose your product framework.

Step 3: Choose a title that sells.

Step 4: Build your table of contents.

Step 5: Create your content.

Step 1: Choose the Role You Are Playing

Whatever product you choose to create, as the author you will essentially be telling a story. To do so you'll need to choose the role you wish to play when delivering your content:

- *Expert*. Here's what I've done, and here's my theory on why it works. This is the role that I chose as the author of this book.
- *Interviewer*. Compile information from other experts. You can compile a product by interviewing others who are experts in their respective fields. A good example of that is Mitch Meyerson's book, *Success Secrets of the Online Marketing Superstars*. He interviewed more than 20 of the best-known online marketing experts in the world and compiled their interviews into a book. (Yours truly is included.)
- *Researcher*. Go out and gather information to serve the needs and desires of your target market. Compile the results to create a product that meets those needs and desires. Research can turn you into an expert at a future date. Jim Collins's book, *Good to Great*, is a perfect example. It's a research study, and it has made him an authority on creating great results in large corporations. You don't need to do a 10-year clinical study as Mr. Collins did, but the concept is the same.
- *Repurposer*. Use and modify existing content (with permission) for a different purpose. Many of the Guerilla Marketing books are excellent examples of this. Jay Conrad Levinson created the Guerilla Marketing brand, and then many other authors co-opted that material and offered it for a different purpose—for example, *Guerrilla Marketing for Job Hunters* by David Perry. (I contributed to this book as well.)

2.7.3 Written Exercise: Which role most appeals to you or is most appropriate to your product or program, and why?

Step 2: Choose Your Product Framework

You'll need a framework in which to organize and present your content. A framework will make it easier not only for you to develop your content but also for your potential client to understand it and get the greatest possible value from it.

You may find that your content is ideally suited to a particular framework. If, for example, you're developing content for a book on pregnancy, the chronological framework may be the logical choice. However, your content may work well in more than one framework. Often an information product or program uses a combination of two or more of the frameworks. Here are six of the most common ones:

1. *Problem/Solution*. State a problem and then present solutions to the problem. *The Magic of Conflict: Turning Your Life of Work into a Work of Art* by Thomas F. Crum is written in this framework. He presents a number of problems that people face in their life and at work and presents solutions to those problems using the philosophical principles of the martial art of *Aikido*.
2. *Numerical*. Create your product as a series of keys or lessons. A well-known example of this would be Stephen Covey's *The 7 Habits of Highly Effective People*.
3. *Chronological*. Some products need to be presented in a particular order because that is the only way it would make sense. Step A must come before Step B, as in *Your Pregnancy Week by Week* by Glade B. Curtis and Judith Schuler.
4. *Modular*. This book is a perfect example. The book consists of three modules: Your Foundation, Building Trust and Credibility, and The Book Yourself Solid 7 Core Self-Promotion Strategies. Within each module are additional tracks presented in a chronological framework. So you see that the book has both a main framework (modular) and a secondary framework (chronological).
5. *Compare/Contrast*. Showcase your creation in terms of presenting several scenarios or options and then compare and contrast them.

Jim Collins, in his book *Good to Great*, compares and contrasts successful and not-so-successful companies.

6. *Reference*. Reference is just as it sounds. You may be creating a product that becomes a valuable resource to members of your target market. A compilation of information is best showcased in a reference format like that in *Words that Sell* by Richard Bayan. It's a reference guide of good words and phrases that help sell.

2.7.4 Written Exercise: Which framework will you choose and why?

Step 3: Choose a Title That Sells

The title of your product or program can make a big difference in whether your product sells. It's the title that initially catches consumers' attention and determines whether they look any further. Your title must be compelling enough for the prospect to want to know more. The consumer should be able to know exactly what you're offering by reading or hearing your title. Investing time to craft a captivating title can have a significant impact on your bottom line. Here are six types of titles that you can adapt to your needs:

1. Suspense: *The Secret Life of Stay-at-Home Moms*
2. Tell a story: *The Path of the Successful Entrepreneur*
3. Address a pain or a fear: *The Top 10 Fears Every Leader Has and How to Overcome Them*
4. Grab the reader's attention. *Caught! The Six Deadliest Dating Mistakes!*
5. Solutions to problems: *Focus: The Seven Keys to Getting Things Done Even If You Have ADD*
6. Emotional connection. *What My Son's Tragedy Taught Me about Living Life to the Fullest*

> **2.7.5 Written Exercise:** Choose one of the title types that fits your product or that you find especially appealing, and brainstorm a number of different title ideas. Have fun with this. Just get your creative juices flowing.

Step 4: Build Your Table of Contents

Your table of contents is another key piece in organizing your content so that it's easy for you to present and easy for your potential clients to understand and follow. Regardless of which role you present your content in, the creation of a product gives the impression that you are an expert, and this is how your target market will view you.

The table of contents should be very well organized and professional. It should be easy to scan through your table of contents to gain an understanding of the concept and the main points. Creating a table of contents also allows you to break your content into manageable pieces. The thought of writing even a simple article, e-book, special report, or book may at first glance seem overwhelming, but it doesn't have to be. Use your table of contents to break the process down into smaller steps that will be much easier and less intimidating to work on.

> **2.7.6 Written Exercise:** Create your table of contents. Keep the following questions in mind:
>
> - What are the steps in understanding your content?
> - Is the flow logical and easy to understand?

Step 5: Create Your Content

Using your table of contents, create a schedule for completing the first draft of each section. Don't let this become overwhelming—it doesn't have to be. If you write as little as a paragraph or two a day, you could have your content for your product or program completed in as little as a week for an e-course or a month or two for a more in-depth product or program.

A Necessary Step in Your Business Development

Creating a product or program is a powerful—and possibly necessary—step in your business development. When you do so your business has the potential to skyrocket. One product will turn into another and another—the possibilities are endless.

Just imagine this: You open your e-mail first thing in the morning and you see 15 new orders—one from Switzerland, one from Australia, one from India, and a dozen from all over the United States—all for the product you recently made available on the Web. It's 7:00 A.M., you're still sipping your first cup of coffee and only half awake, and you've already earned $3,479.27.

While this scenario may seem more like a dream than reality to you right now, it's entirely possible to achieve, and it's much easier to do than you might imagine; just follow the steps I've outlined above for creating an unlimited number of information products on virtually any topic you can think of! Before you know it you'll be hearing the beautiful, melodic *ka-ching, ka-ching* sound of your web site-turned-cash-register as the orders come rolling in.

8

Super Simple Selling

The jungle is dark but full of diamonds . . .

—Arthur Miller

As a service provider you may not want to think of yourself as a salesperson. You're in the business of helping others, and the sales process may feel contradictory to your core purpose. If you're uncomfortable with the sales process, it's likely that you view it as unethical, manipulative, and dishonest. Looking at it that way, who wouldn't be uncomfortable?

Many service professionals also feel uncomfortable charging for services that either come easily to them or that they love doing. There is often a sense that if it comes easily and is enjoyable, there's something wrong with charging others for doing it.

Add the fact that service professionals sell themselves as much as they sell a product, and the whole idea becomes even more uncomfortable. It may feel like you're bragging and being shamelessly immodest.

Becoming comfortable with the sales process requires that you let go of any limiting beliefs you may have about being worthy of the money you're earning and requires a shift in your perspective of the sales process itself.

Let Go of Limiting Beliefs

Most people who are successful get paid to do what they do well. You don't become successful doing something that you find difficult. You become successful when you exploit your natural talents. Imagine Tom Hanks saying he shouldn't get paid to do movies because he's really good at it and loves it. Or Alex Rodriguez saying he should play baseball for free because it's so easy and he enjoys it.

Tom Hanks, A-Rod, and anyone else you can think of who is, or was, wildly successful at what they do, work to the bone at becoming even better at what they are naturally gifted at doing. They create extraordinary experiences for the people they serve, whether it's an audience, a fan, or a client. That's why they—and you—deserve to be paid top dollar.

If you've been feeling like you can't, or shouldn't, be paid to do what you love, you must let that limiting belief go if you're to be booked solid.

If you don't believe you are worth what you are charging, it is unlikely that a lot of people are going to hire you based on those fees. You need to resonate fully with the prices you are quoting so that others will resonate with them as well. To do so, you may need to work on shifting your beliefs so that you feel more comfortable with charging higher fees, rather than lowering your fees to eliminate the discomfort.

There is an old joke about a guy who gets into a cab in New York City and asks the driver how to get to Carnegie Hall, and the driver responds, "Practice, practice, practice." You're going to increase your resonance with practice. It's just like practicing a martial art, or a sport, or singing. Singing is a great example because your voice becomes more resonant the more you practice. At first it's uncomfortable, but over time it becomes easier and more natural. This will happen when you quote your fees. Once you're comfortable quoting your fees, other people will feel that comfort and that energetic resonance, and they'll happily pay you what you're worth.

Shifting Your Perspective

The book yourself solid paradigm of sales is all about building relationships with your potential clients based on trust. It is, quite simply, about having a sincere conversation that allows you to let your potential clients know what you can do to help them. You aren't manipulating or coercing people into buying something they have no real need or desire to buy. You're making them aware of something you offer that they already need, want, or desire.

Thinking in terms of solutions and benefits is the *ah-ha* to the selling process. It's the key to shifting your perspective. It's so foolproof you'll never think of the selling process the same way again.

When you think in terms of solutions and problems solved, clients will beg to work with you. You are a consultant, a lifelong advisor. When you have fundamental solutions and a desire to help others, it becomes your moral imperative to show and tell as many people as possible. You are changing lives!

Where Are the Hot Buttons?

Selling is based on pure emotion. Have you ever heard the term *hot buttons*? These are emotional triggers, the ones that will get straight to the heart of our pleasures, our panics, our pains. These hot-topic personal issues pave the way for the emotional path of selling. Here are a few generic emotional triggers almost everyone has:

- People want to feel accepted and needed.
- People want to feel satisfaction from their accomplishments.
- People want to feel admired and recognized for their accomplishments.

Please note: Hot buttons should not be mistaken for manipulation. You cannot create a hot button for someone. Your potential clients respond to the issue you're uncovering because it creates an emotion pull and a positive charge for them.

Problems, Predicaments, and Dilemmas

We all have problems from time to time. Even if you tend to be an optimistic person, the norm when sharing problems, predicaments, and dilemmas with others is to focus on the negative. Unfortunately, doing so isn't an effective way to resolve them. I'm sure you already know this, but complete Written Exercise 2.8.1 to see what effect a negative focus has on an already problematic situation.

2.8.1 Written Exercise: Identify a small problem that you have in your life right now (nothing too big). Answer the following:

- What is the problem, predicament, or dilemma?
- How long has this been a problem?
- How have you failed to correct it in the past?
- Why is it impossible to fully correct the situation?

Now that you've answered those questions, are you feeling motivated to take action to resolve your problem? No? That's not surprising. I'll bet you feel even more discouraged or deflated about the issue than you were before. You may even feel like the situation is hopeless.

The questions in Written Exercise 2.8.1 focus on the negative, on the problem itself, what you've been doing wrong, and why the situation is unlikely to change. Placing your attention on the negative drains your energy, robs you of your power, and keeps you stuck.

Place Your Attention on the Positive

No matter how negative or difficult a problem may seem, you can choose to place your attention on the positive. Let's look at the same problem you identified earlier but from a more positive perspective.

2.8.2 Written Exercise: Answer the following:

1. What are you working on? Or what is your goal? State it in the positive and within your control. Clearly define the goal and think about a specific time frame within which to achieve it.
2. How will you know when you have achieved it? Use all your senses and visualize the results. Imagine how you would really feel and how different your interactions with others would be.
   - What results will you see?
   - What feedback will you hear?
   - What feelings will you have?
3. What are the benefits of going after this outcome? If you go after this outcome and accomplish what you set out to do, what will you gain? Be specific. Will any of your relationships change? Will you sleep more peacefully at night? Will the confidence you gain from achieving this goal affect other areas of your life?
4. If you reach this outcome, what will it be worth to you?
5. Do the benefits outweigh the perceived costs?

How are you feeling now, having looked at the same problem from a different perspective? When you place your attention on the positive, on what you want rather than on what you don't want, on all the many benefits of making a change and the positive outcome you'll achieve, you raise your energy, empower yourself, and are inspired to make positive changes.

The Super Simple Selling System

The purpose of the previous exercises was to allow you to experience for yourself the impact that a shift in perspective can have on a situation. Through the Book Yourself Solid Super Simple Selling System you will learn to do the same for your potential clients.

It's time to stop thinking about selling as a canned presentation that influences or manipulates someone. The selling process is more about your clients and less about you. If you are selling properly, here's all you really need to do:

- Ask more questions than you answer.
- Listen more than you speak.
- Consider the needs and desires of your potential clients before considering your own.
- Keep the conversation positive and empowering.

With the Book Yourself Solid Super Simple Selling System you will initiate conversations with your potential clients using the questions asked in Written Exercise 2.8.2. Using these questions in a genuine and sincere conversation will allow you to guide your potential clients to view any problem from a positive perspective. While they may have gone through the usual moan-and-groan session about a problem with friends, family, and business associates—and been left feeling discouraged and defeated—after having a conversation with you they'll walk away feeling uplifted and empowered to take action and make positive life changes.

You may be asking, "How is that a simple selling system? How is that going to help me to sell myself and my services?" That's the beauty of the Book Yourself Solid Super Simple Selling System—you're simply helping your potential clients to feel better about themselves and their lives by showing them that they can take control and make changes. The conversation becomes a super simple selling system with the addition of just one key question: *Would you like a partner to help you achieve these goals?* With that one question you make yourself the key to the solution.

It's as simple as that! Can you see the benefits of this selling process? Your clients do all the selling for you. They…

- Articulate the benefits.
- Create mental imagery toward producing results.
- Keep their self-criticisms out of the way.

- Visualize results and gain confidence about what their life would look like.
- Visualize you as the right partner to help them achieve these goals.

Shifting your perspective brings great results, and if you can help your clients to shift their perspective they'll love you because they'll start seeing and living those amazing results for themselves.

2.8.3 Booked Solid Action Step: Practice without pressure. Try this process with a good friend and see what happens. Focus on:

- Letting your friend share his story.
- Listening to the meaning behind the words.
- Asking yourself what the needs are that are deeper than the words he speaks.
- Identifying his hot buttons or emotional triggers.

Once you start getting comfortable with the super simple selling system, go for it! Don't limit yourself. Next time you talk with clients, ask your questions with confidence and let them find their own solutions in working with you. Remember, if a client says no, or doesn't say yes, don't take it personally. Don't assume you did something wrong. Try to avoid acting out of defensiveness. What is actually happening is that the client still has unanswered questions. Once you find out what they are and answer them, then you can start working together.

This is truly where you learn all the good stuff. When you hear a no, you get a green light to dig deeper and find the true objection. And there probably isn't just one. You may uncover a handful. And every time you uncover and answer one, you may find another. If this is your experience, congratulate yourself. You are equipped with wonderful information and moving toward lots of opportunities to book yourself solid.

Visualize the Outcome

Let's switch gears to talk about the power of positive thinking and visualizing the outcome you want. Thirty seconds of visualization will change your entire conversation!

Try this mental exercise: Before you speak with clients, visualize the word *yes* coming out of their mouths. Hear them say it in your head and . . .

- See a smile of agreement.
- Watch their expression become light and happy.
- Visualize them writing you a check for your full fee.

This might sound a little silly, but I promise that if you set your intention and outcome, you will absolutely change your results for the better. Don't just trust me on this one, try it. Take a mini-leap of faith and experience the results for yourself. I can tell you so many examples in my life where this changed the course of a conversation. It is not a far-fetched theory—it's a very real possibility.

The Super Simple Selling System Made Even Simpler

If this super simple selling system is too much for you to take in all at once, use the superduper simple selling system to book new clients and realize immediate results:

- *Inquire:* What is your goal?
- *Show* the benefits after they reach the goal.
- *Offer:* Would you like a partner to help you with that?

That's it. Make this superduper simple selling system your mantra and you'll be fast on your way to being booked solid.

Keep in Touch

For a next step, get a commitment. Again, think of yourself as a lifelong consultant. You wouldn't be doing the best thing for the client if you remained silent, so let your light shine and give an action plan. Here are some tips to remember:

- Move the relationship forward.
- Follow up and ask for small commitments.
- Don't give in and don't give up if you know you can help.

The good news is that eventually the benefits you provide will someday be a priority. Something in your clients' life will change. If you haven't kept in contact with them and followed up, they'll look to someone else to help them reach their goals. But if you have called, cared, and followed up, if you've let the Book Yourself Solid Sales Cycle work its magic, you'll be the one waiting in the wings to work with them.

These are the lovely, easy steps to simple selling and booking yourself solid. Start small, end big, and remember—successful selling is really nothing more than showing your potential clients how you can help them to live a happier, more successful life.

The Book Yourself Solid 7 Core Self-Promotion Strategies

By now I think you understand why most service professionals hate the idea of marketing and selling. They don't have a foundation for their business, nor have they developed a strategy for building trust and credibility. Now that you've diligently worked through Modules One and Two, you have a foundation for your business, and you have a strategy for building trust and credibility. Watch out, because you're not only on your way to liking marketing and selling but dangerously close to loving both.

By the time you complete Module Three, you'll be in a full-on, mad, passionate love affair not only with the idea of marketing and selling but also with the real-world application of the Book Yourself Solid 7 Core Self-Promotion Strategies.

Just like any new love affair, you want to blend with the newness of it all. Don't let the multitude of strategies, techniques, and exercises in

Module Three overwhelm you. Pick the strategies that are most aligned with your strengths and run with them. The only possible mistake you can make is to try all of these strategies at once. If you do, you run the risk of watering down your efforts, becoming frustrated with the results, or worse, quitting before you see any results. Remember, any one of these techniques can seriously book you solid, and you'll build a successful business full of wonderful, energetic people.

Enjoy, embrace, and profit from the Book Yourself Solid 7 Core Self-Promotion Strategies:

1. The Book Yourself Solid Networking Strategy.
2. The Book Yourself Solid Direct Outreach Strategy.
3. The Book Yourself Solid Referral Strategy.
4. The Book Yourself Solid Web Strategy.
5. The Book Yourself Solid Speaking and Demonstrating Strategy.
6. The Book Yourself Solid Writing Strategy.
7. The Book Yourself Solid Keep-In-Touch Strategy.

The concepts and action steps laid out in the following pages will help you create relentless demand for the services and products you offer to energetically build a cadre of high-value, high-paying, inspiring clients.

9

The Book Yourself Solid Networking Strategy

Some cause happiness wherever they go; others, whenever they go.
—Oscar Wilde

Networking, Ugh!

It's possible that—like the thought of marketing and sales—the thought of networking may make you cringe. When most service professionals hear the word *networking*, they think of the old-school business mentality of promotional networking at meet-and-greet events where everyone is there to schmooze and manipulate one another in an attempt to gain some advantage for themselves or their business.

Who wouldn't cringe at the thought of spending an hour or two exchanging banalities and sales pitches with a phony smile plastered on your face to hide your discomfort? If it feels uncomfortable, self-serving, and deceptive, chances are all those business cards you collected will end up in a drawer of your desk never to be seen again because you'll so dread following up that you'll procrastinate until they're forgotten.

Take heart, dear reader! It doesn't have to be that way! The Book

117

Yourself Solid Networking Strategy operates from an entirely different perspective; it's all about connecting and sharing with others. All that's necessary is to shift your perspective from one of scarcity and fear to one of abundance and love. With the Book Yourself Solid Networking Strategy, the focus is on sincerely and freely giving and sharing, and by doing so, building and deepening mutually beneficial relationships with others. It's all about making lasting connections.

Making the Shift to the Book Yourself Solid Way

The first step is to change your perspective of what networking really is. Do you believe that networking has something to do with the old-school business mentality of scarcity and fear that asks:

- How can I push my agenda?
- How can I get or keep the attention on myself?
- What can I say to really impress or manipulate?
- How can I use each contact to get what I want or need?
- How can I crush the competition?
- How can I dominate the marketplace?

The Book Yourself Solid Networking Strategy (one of abundance and love) asks:

- What can I give and offer to others?
- How can I help others to be successful?
- How can I start and continue friendly conversations?
- How can I put others at ease?
- How can I best express my sincerity and generosity?
- How can I listen attentively so as to recognize the needs and desires of others?
- How can I provide true value to others?

- How can I fully express myself so I can make genuine connections with others?

Let's replace *networking* with the word *connecting*. Does that help you fall in love with the concept of networking? We don't get contacts, we don't find contacts, we don't have contacts; we make *connections* with real people.

> *A connection with another human being means that you're in sync with, and relevant to, each other. Let that be our definition of networking.*

When people ask me what has been the most important factor in my rapid success as a service professional, I always have a two-word answer: other people. My marketing success is determined by other people—how they respond to me and I respond to them and what opportunities we can create for each other. Your marketing success is also determined by other people.

If you keep asking yourself the value-added questions above and follow the Book Yourself Solid Networking Strategy that I'm about to present to you, you'll create a large and powerful network built on compassion, trust, and integrity, a network that is priceless and will reap rewards for years to come.

The Book Yourself Solid 50/50 Networking Rule

The Book Yourself Solid Networking Strategy employs the 50/50 networking rule, which requires that we share our networking focus evenly between potential clients and other professionals. Most people think of networking as something you do primarily to try to reel in clients. That's not so.

While the Book Yourself Solid Networking Strategy adds value to the lives of people who could become your clients, you'll also want to spend 50 percent of your networking time connecting with other professionals. Networking with other professionals provides you with an opportunity to connect and share resources, knowledge, and information. Bear in mind that working solo does not mean working alone. You can create so much more value when other talented people are involved.

Have You Got Any Soul?

The absolute best education I have ever received on the concept of networking was from Tim Sanders in his book, *Love Is the Killer App: How to Win Business and Influence Friends.*

Sanders' message is that being a *lovecat* is the key to business success, and it's at the heart of the Book Yourself Solid Networking Strategy. Sanders quotes philosopher and writer Milton Mayeroff's definition of love from his book *On Caring*: "Love is the selfless promotion of the growth of the other." Sanders then defines his idea of business love as "the act of intelligently and sensibly sharing your intangibles with your bizpartners."

What are those intangibles? According to Sanders, they are your knowledge, your network, and your compassion. They are the essential keys to networking success.

Networking requires that you consciously integrate each of these intangibles until they become a natural part of your daily life, everywhere you go, and in everything you do. Yes, I said *daily life*. Networking isn't something you do only at networking events. It's an ongoing process that will bring terrific benefits.

Share *What* You Know, *Whom* You Know, and *How* You Feel

- *Share what you know.* This means everything you've learned—whether through life experience, observation, conversation, or study—and everything you continue to learn.

- *Share whom you know.* This is everyone you know. It's as simple as that. Whether family, friend, or business associate, everyone in your network is potentially a good connection with someone else, and you never know whom you might meet next who will be the other half of a great connection.
- *Share how you feel.* This is all of your compassion, the quality that makes us most human. It's our ability to empathize with others. Sharing your compassion in every aspect of your life will bring the greatest rewards, not only for your bottom-line but in knowing that you're operating from your heart and your integrity in all your interactions.

Note: Give each of these three intangibles freely and with no expectation of return. While it may seem calculated to plan a strategy around them, the fact remains that when you're smart, friendly, and helpful, people will like you, will enjoy being around you, and will remember you when they or someone they know needs your services.

Sharing and Increasing What You Know

I recommend books all the time, and I'm often asked, "How do you read so much?" which always makes me smile because, when I was a kid, my father was worried that I wasn't going to amount to much because he couldn't get me to read much beyond the Hardy Boys. But now I read about two books per month. What changed? I realized that the answers to every single question I have are offered in a book. Even better, I get to choose what I learn and from whom. Then armed with this information, I am in a great place to share it with others.

You may be thinking, "But if I'm always referring to other people's work, won't they just forget about me and get everything they need from the book or resource I referenced?" Good question! First of all, if they love the book or information that you referred them to, it's highly likely they'll associate that value with you. They will feel connected to you because you helped them achieve a goal or change their life or simply learn something new, the value of which is not to be underestimated. The more knowledgeable you are, and are perceived to be, the more trust and credibility you'll build in your network. Reading books is, by far, the best and most efficient way to increase your knowledge.

Reading a book on a topic that is related to the services you provide offers an easy way to start a conversation with potential clients or contacts. In fact, they may start the conversation with you instead with one simple question, "What are you reading?" I realized this gem of a networking technique by accident. I was born and raised in New York, where almost every New Yorker rides the subway. It's simply the best way to get around. It's also one of the best places to make new friends. Think about it; you're constantly bumped, pushed, and shoved by people you don't know. So instead of fighting all the time, most New Yorkers decide the path of least resistance is simply to strike up a conversation. If you have a book in your hand, what do you think this conversation is going to be about? You guessed it—the book. And what better way to get into your Book Yourself Solid Dialogue than to explain why you're reading the particular book you're holding in your hand.

Of course, this doesn't just apply to New York subway cars. Everywhere you go you're running into, meeting, and connecting with other people. What if you always had a book in your hand that allowed you to share what you know about your particular area of expertise, for the betterment of the person you're talking with? I know that not every person you meet or run into is a member of your target market, or at first thought, can send you clients, but it doesn't matter. You're just finding opportunities to add value to those you meet by sharing what you know.

3.9.1 Booked Solid Action Step: Try it with this book. Carry it wherever you go and explain to people why you're reading it. You'll have the opportunity to talk about the Book Yourself Solid philosophy of giving so much value that you think you've gone too far and then giving more, and how it's in sync with your values and what you do. You'll then be able to get into your Book Yourself Solid Dialogue.

Ask yourself what knowledge, once acquired, would add the greatest value and make you more attractive to potential clients and business partners, and then go after learning it. Your investment in books—buying them and reading them—will pay dividends you can't even imagine. In fact, in *Love Is the Killer App*, Sanders describes a wonderful system for reading, comprehending, and applying your newfound knowledge to help you make deeper connections with others in business.

3.9.2 Written Exercise: List five books you've read that you know are must-reads for your target market. Think about and jot down the names of any specific people who come to mind for each book.

3.9.3 Written Exercise: List five books that have been recommended to you as must-reads or that you know contain information that would add value to your target market. Then go out and make the investment in at least one this week.

If you'd like my extensive list of recommended reading, go to www.Book YourselfSolid.com and click on Free Resources.

3.9.4 Written Exercise: Books aren't our only source of knowledge. As I mentioned earlier, our life experience, observations, and conversations are all sources of knowledge as well. Think about the many areas you're knowledgeable about and list a minimum of five. Have fun with this and just let it flow. If you know a lot about skydiving, or *ikebana* (the Japanese art of flower arranging), include it! You never know what subject might help make a connection.

Share Whom You Know

I will do anything I can to get business for people I like and respect. Last year I sent over $100,000 worth of referrals to one of my web designers. I go out of my way to serve the people who serve me.

Think about it: Whom do you want to give your business to or recommend to other members of your network? It's the people who have served you in some way; the people who are friendly, nice, smart, and helpful; the people who will go the extra mile, give that little bit more than anyone expects, and who genuinely strive to provide the best service they can with integrity. It's the people who are upbeat, always have a ready smile, and from whom you walk away feeling supported and energized.

If you are that person in each and every interaction you have with others, whether business or personal, your network is going to grow exponentially, and those people are going to remember you and want to do business with you. They're going to link you with others in their network with whom you can make beneficial connections, and they're going to refer you to everyone they know who could possibly use your service or products.

I can think of scores, if not hundreds, of friends and colleagues I have who are like this. There is one who comes to mind as the ideal example of what it really means to share your network openly, without reservation, and without expecting anything in return.

Caroline Kohles, of www.NiaNewYork.com, is a fitness, health, and wellness expert. She is one of the most authentic and talented people I have the pleasure of knowing, and I will do anything for her any chance I get. Why? Because she constantly sends me clients, connects me with people that I can partner with, gives me opportunities to market my services, and constantly shares things she's learned or heard about that she thinks will help me personally or professionally. The most remarkable thing about Caroline is that she expects nothing in return.

There is one thing that is essential to consider with respect to sharing your network. You must do what you say you're going to do—always. And if you don't, apologize and make it right. If you make commitments and don't fulfill them, you'll damage your reputation and close doorways that were once open to you. If you don't make commitments to connect, no one will do it for you. These habits of commitment making and fulfilling are essential to developing yourself into a masterful connector who truly and meaningfully adds value to the lives of others.

3.9.5 Written Exercise: First list five people in your network who consistently support you by sending referrals, giving you advice, or doing anything else that's helpful. Then identify someone in your network for each of these five people that you could connect them with. Whom do you know who will add value to their work or life? Is it a potential client, a potential business partner, a potential vendor?

The people you listed in Written Exercise 3.9.5 are going to appreciate the opportunity to connect or the recommendation that you make, and when someone they know needs your service or product, they'll be more likely to remember you and to reciprocate.

Remember, too, that the six degrees of separation theory says that you are only six people away from the person or information you need. (In your field, your degrees of separation from anyone you need or want to connect with are even fewer.) Everyone you meet has the potential to connect you (through his network and his contacts' networks) to someone or some piece of information that you need. So step out of your comfort zone and make a sincere effort to connect with people you might not normally interact with. The more diverse your network of connections, the more powerful and effective your network becomes. It opens doors that might otherwise remain closed.

3.9.6 Written Exercise: Think of the types of people or professions that are *not* represented in your current network. List five that would expand and benefit your network, as well as ideas for where you might find them.

Share How You Feel

In the service business people will generally not hire you unless they feel you have compassion for what they're going through. Expressing that compassion is the first step to a successful working relationship. How do you do that? Listen attentively. Be fully present when making connections, smile as often as possible, make eye contact, and ask engaging, open-ended questions that express your curiosity and interest.

Take the time to add value to the person you're connecting with by offering information or resources that speak to her needs. If you don't have what she needs, think about who in your network would meet her needs and how to go about acting as the link for them. Remember, this is done with no expectation of any immediate return.

3.9.7 Written Exercise: Note a recent situation, business or personal, when someone else expressed compassion for you. Think about how you felt following the interaction. How do you feel about that person because of the compassion he or she showed for you?

Networking Opportunities

The possibilities for networking opportunities are endless. Any time you're sharing your connections, knowledge, and compassion, you're networking. Any time you're learning more about what others do and know, you're networking. Anytime you link or connect two people you know, you're networking.

Informal Networking Opportunities

These are the ones that we might not think of as networking but that we can't afford to overlook. We have dozens of these every day:

- Casual chat in line at the grocery store.
- While checking out videos at your local video store.
- Speaking with your neighbor while walking your dog.

Let's take the manager at the video store as an example. Every weekend you stop by the local video store to pick up movies. Each time, you smile and chat with the manager as he checks out your movies. After a while you begin to greet one another by name, and you know enough about him to ask after his family. He mentions he was looking forward to a special evening out with his wife the following night for their anniversary but then sighs and says, "But our babysitter canceled at the last minute. I wish [one of the phrases to always be listening for] that I knew of a good backup to call." You just happen to have this amazing babysitter you can always count on in a pinch. You pull out your PDA, look up her number, and give her a call. "Sally, meet Bob. He's looking for a great sitter for tomorrow night, and you're the best, so of course I thought of you," you say as you hand your cell phone to Bob.

Now this exchange has absolutely nothing to do with business, or does it? On the surface it has nothing to do with business. However, whom do you think either Bob or Sally is going to call when they, or someone they know, need your service? Bob is thrilled with you because you've saved his special night out. Sally is thrilled with you because you've given her high praise and new business. Both of them feel better following their interaction with you, and that makes you memorable. And most important, you've increased your connection factor with each of them. Your connection factor is how much trust you've built with each person in your network. The more value you add to a person's life, the more he or she is going to trust you.

3.9.8 Written Exercise: Think for a moment: Have you recently missed any opportunities for making a deeper connection with someone? List five connections that would have been made if you had just shared your knowledge, your network, or your compassion.

Online Networking Opportunities

There are numerous ways to network these days without even having to leave your house—some formal, some informal. Here are just a few:

- Business networking web sites such as LinkedIn.com, Meetup.com, Ryze.com, Monster.com.

- Online discussion groups and forums: Yahoo groups, Google groups, MSN groups.
- Any interactive web site where you can connect with others, such as membership clubs and learning programs.

Check out http://OnlineBusinessNetworks.com for more information on business networking sites and how to maximize use of them. Do a web search for *online business networking*, or come on over to www.BookYourself Solid.com. We have a free networking forum that's dedicated to helping service professionals connect with each other and set up referral groups and so much more.

3.9.9 Written Exercise: List three places online where you can start to raise your personal and professional profile by adding value to others.

Formal Networking Opportunities

These are the more formal, business meet-and-greet opportunities that can be fun and enjoyable and offer great rewards:

- Toastmasters International.
- Chamber of Commerce meetings.
- Networking/leads groups—for example, Business Network International.
- Trade association meetings.

3.9.10 Written Exercise: Do some research and come up with three additional business networking opportunities like the ones I've listed that you can attend with the intention of adding value to others as well as enhancing your network.

Networking Events—What to Do

- *Do arrive on time.* This is not the time to stage a grand entrance by being fashionably late or to tell any stories about why you're late. Nobody cares. If you're late and it's noticed, apologize and leave it at that.

- *Do relax and be yourself.* Contrary to conventional wisdom, you don't have to fit in. It may sound trite, but be yourself, unless when you're being yourself you end the evening with your tie wrapped around your head doing a nosedive into the shrimp salad. Seriously, people want to meet the person who is out in front, who is writing the rules and taking the lead, not the one who is following the pack. So don't be afraid to be fully self-expressed. If you are you'll be more memorable.

- *Do smile and be friendly.* Both men and women may worry that smiling too big will be construed as some sort of a come-on or that they're desperate for attention. This fear of being misunderstood will hold you back. Let it go! Better to err on the side of a big, friendly smile than to be considered unfriendly or standoffish.

- *Do focus on giving.* If your focus is on giving of yourself, you're going to get returns in spades. If you focus on what you can get, you will be much less successful.

- *Do prepare for the event.* Learn the names of the organizers and some of the key players. Identify what and how you can share with others at the function: whom you know (without being a name dropper), what you know (without being a know-it-all), and what you can share from your heart (without making assumptions) with the people who will be at this particular event. You never know what might change someone's life.

- *Do introduce yourself to the person hosting the event.* This person may be a very valuable addition to your network. Never forget to say, "Thank you."

- *Do introduce yourself to the bigwig.* If there's someone you want to meet at a big seminar or event, someone famous in your industry, do you go up to her and say, "Here's what I do and here's my business card"? No! You start by offering praise. You say, "I just want to tell you your work had a great effect on me," or "Your work inspired me to do this or that." Then the next time you are at the same event you might say, "I would just love to hold your coffee cup." Meaning, "I would love to assist you in some way that would add value to your life or work." She may say, "I don't think so," but what have you got to lose? Then again, she may respond by saying, "Yeah, you seem like a really genuine and considerate person. I've got some stuff you can do." Don't forget that successful and busy people always have more on their plate than they can reasonably handle. They're always looking for talented people to help make their life easier. If you can help reduce someone's stress level, you've made a friend for life.

- *Do offer something when first meeting someone, whenever possible.* Offer praise (as in the above example), compassion, or a connection. When you can say, "I know someone you've got to meet," or "There's a great book I think may offer the solution to your problem," he is going to see you very differently from the person who shoved a business card in his face and said, "Let's stay in touch, Dude." If you can leave him feeling even better, more uplifted, and energized after his interaction with you, he's going to remember you.

- *Do start conversations by asking questions.* This is a great approach, especially if you're nervous. It takes the spotlight off of you and allows the other person to shine. It allows you to learn something new at the same time.

- *Do identify two or three things you'd like to learn from the people at the function.* People are drawn to others who are curious and interested.

- *Do make eye contact.* It expresses respect and interest in the person you're speaking with. And stay focused on the person you're speaking with. If you're speaking with me, but your eyes are constantly scanning the room for someone more important or relevant to you, don't you think it might make me feel unappreciated?

- *Do wear comfortable clothing.* If you're constantly fidgeting or worrying about how you look in clothes that aren't comfortable or don't fit properly, you'll be self-conscious and others will sense it.

- *Do take the initiative.* Go up to people and make friends. People love to be asked about themselves, their hobbies, or their family. This is the time to get to know a few personal tidbits that will give you the opportunity to find a common interest that makes connecting easier and more natural.

- *Do offer a firm handshake.* Hold your drink in your left hand. This eliminates the need to wipe your damp hand on your clothes before shaking hands. And, guys, don't think you need to shake hands differently with a woman than you do with a man. A firm handshake (not a death grip) is always appropriate.

- *Do be inclusive.* Ask others to join your conversations; this is very important. Don't monopolize people, especially those who are in high demand, like the speaker from the event. It makes the speaker uncomfortable. Remember, she's there to meet lots of people too. It also annoys others who want to meet the person you're trying to keep to yourself. Tip: If you want to be helpful, ask the speaker if there is anybody you can introduce her to, or simply be sure to keep including people in your conversations with her. This way, you'll be seen as a very generous and open person by the others at the event, and the speaker will remember you as someone who helped her easily network and navigate the event.

- *Do ask for a business card and then keep in touch.* It's your responsibility to ask for a card if you want one, and it's your responsibility to follow up. Quality not quantity counts when making genuine personal connections. If you race through an event passing out and collecting business cards from anyone and everyone as though there were a prize for the most cards gained at the end of the event, you'll do yourself a huge disservice. And remember, just because someone gives you his business card does *not* mean you have permission to add him to your mailing list or e-zine list. You do not. You can certainly send a personal e-mail as a follow up, and you should, but you should not and cannot add him to your list. You don't have permission to do so. This is a pet peeve of mine. At least 25 percent of the time I'm asked for my business card at a conference, I end up on another newsletter list. That's not cool.

- *Do have a pen with you always.* When you receive a business card, write a little note about any commitment to follow up, what you talked about, any personal bits or unusual things that will help you to remember the person and to personalize future contact, and be sure to include the date and name of the function where you met.

Networking Events—What Not to Do

- *Don't try to be cool.* And don't overcompensate for your nervousness by bragging about your success; this is a major turn-off.
- *Don't let "What do you do?" be the first question you ask.* Let it come up naturally in conversation.
- *Don't sit with people you know for the majority of the event.* While it may be more comfortable to sit with the people you know, it becomes too easy to stay with them, and if you do, you'll defeat the purpose of being there. Step out of your comfort zone and get to know new people.
- *Don't juggle multiple items.* Travel light to eliminate the necessity of juggling your coat, purse, briefcase, drink, or buffet plate. Keep that right hand free for handshakes and for jotting down quick notes on business cards.
- *Don't complain about networking or the event you're attending.* Don't complain about anything. The cycle of complaining is easy to get drawn into, especially at events where almost everyone is a bit uncomfortable. While complaining is an icebreaker, it's not an attractive one. Change the subject—for example, "Have you tried the shrimp?"—or take the opportunity to recommend this great book, *Book Yourself Solid*, and how it's transformed the way you think about networking events.
- *Don't take yourself too seriously.* Remember to relax and have fun.

You Are Always Networking

Your profits will come from connections with people who can send you business—whether that's by way of a satisfied client who refers others to you; or another professional who has the ability to book you for speaking engagements, write about you, or partner with you; or the manager at the video store who appreciates your big, friendly smile each weekend and the recommendation you made for a great baby-sitter when he desperately needed one.

With the Book Yourself Solid Networking Strategy, the prospect of creating a phenomenal network of connections doesn't have to be overwhelming or intimidating. We all network constantly, with everyone, every day. Now we just need to do it consciously, with greater awareness, until doing so becomes a natural and comfortable part of our daily lives.

Then follow up. Keep in touch. It is imperative that you get every one of your connections into your database and act on each connection. If the contact isn't in your database or you don't take the action necessary to keep in touch, your networking is pointless. Have some form of this database with you at all times—PDA, planner, personal address book—so you can instantly connect others rather than having to get back to them.

So You've Got Spinach in Your Teeth

I've given you a lot of techniques in this chapter about what to do, what not to do, and how to interact with others when you're networking, but there's a big difference between techniques and principles, and it's the principles that are most important to remember and begin implementing. If you can incorporate the principles, you'll naturally do well.

For example, everyone says when you meet people at a networking event you're supposed to look them in the eye, give them a firm handshake, smile, and nod your head, but if you do that and don't take the giver's stance, it won't matter how slick you are. However, if you always take the giver's stance and share whom you know, what you know, and how you feel, even if you have spinach in your teeth and your palm is sweaty, you'll be fine, because people are going to respond to who you are. In fact, they'll share their compassion with you by gently letting you know about the large piece of spinach entrenched between your two front teeth.

So what do you think? Are you ready to network your way to more clients, more profit, and deeper connections with people? Sharing your knowledge, your network, and your compassion will bring you one step closer to being booked solid.

10

The Book Yourself
Solid Direct
Outreach Strategy

You miss 100% of the shots you don't take.

—Wayne Gretzky

Ideally, all of your customers and clients will come looking for you. Realistically, there may be times, especially in the beginning, that you'll need to proactively reach out to potential customers and clients and make offers. In addition, there will be many times in your business, but especially when you're just starting out, that you'll want to reach out to other professionals, organizations, and associations to network, cross-promote, and offer your services.

Let's clearly define what direct outreach is *not* before detailing exactly what it is and how to do it authentically, easily, and successfully. It is *not* spam, which I consider unsolicited mail or e-mail of any kind, sent indiscriminately to mailing lists or newsgroups—otherwise known as junk mail. As you know, spam, as defined here, is not the Book Yourself Solid way. It never has been and never will be. Before the advent of the Internet, direct outreach was a very common marketing strategy. I suppose it's no less common today, but unfortunately, it is often perceived as spam. You must be very careful and discerning with respect to how you use the Book Yourself Solid Direct Outreach Strategy.

When initiating your direct outreach strategy, please make sure that your efforts are targeted, individualized, valuable, and legitimate so they are not perceived as spam and instead are appreciated and acted upon.

Using the Book Yourself Solid Direct Outreach Strategy is all about making personal connections. Whichever of the following direct outreach tools you employ, you should be reaching out to others from the heart, in a way that is genuine and authentic for you.

When to Use Direct Outreach

You will find yourself using the Book Yourself Solid Direct Outreach Strategy time and time again when you want to reach out:

- To an ideal client or others within your target market to let them know how you can serve them.
- To the decision maker at an organization or association to cross-promote, secure speaking engagements, submit articles for publication, and more.
- To the press.
- For myriad other business development opportunities.

Direct Outreach Tools

- Letters
- Calls
- E-mail
- Postcards
- Brochures and flyers
- Whatever-it-takes direct outreach

Letters

Letters can be an effective form of direct outreach because people generally still open mail that looks interesting or pertinent, especially when it's hand-written and personalized. When someone sends me a letter with information or an offer that is relevant and timely, I'll take note. Following up is the key to your direct outreach strategy. The letter is a great tool to begin the direct outreach process. You will then follow up with a phone call or e-mail.

The most important aspect of your direct outreach letter is personalization. "Dear Sir/Madam" simply will not do. If you don't at least have the name of the person you're writing to, you might as well move on to your next direct outreach initiative. You must do your homework. Find out everything you can about the person you're trying to connect with. Whom do you know who may know someone who knows them, or better yet, knows them personally?

Start your letter by telling your reader why you're writing. Be friendly and sincere. And then take a moment to flatter your reader. What have you found out about this person in your research that impressed you so much that you want to share it with her? But remember to first tell your reader why you're writing so she'll feel comfortable reading on. She needs to know if it's worth her time to read your letter.

The next step is to expand upon your reason for writing and make your case. According to Seth Godin (*Free Prize Inside!: The Next Big Marketing Idea*), there are three things that others take into account, whether consciously or unconsciously, when they consider a proposal you make:

1. Is it going to be successful?
2. Is it worth doing?
3. Is this person able to do what he says he can?

If you get a resounding "Yes!" for each question, you're in. If your reader raises an eyebrow at even one of the questions, you've probably gone as far as you're going to go with this person. In order for your direct outreach letter— or any other direct outreach tool you use—to be effective, all the questions must be answered in the affirmative. So take an honest, thoughtful approach to reaching out to others.

When I was an actor (that was my first career) I had a modicum of success. I appeared in *Sex & The City*, *Third Watch*, *Law & Order*, *All My Children*, *The Pelican Brief*, *Down to Earth*, and many other shows. I also did hundreds of television commercials and voiceovers but hung up my hat for what I thought was the meaning and stability of a career in the corporate world. Boy was I wrong about that. Anyway, I recall blowing auditions because I was trying to knock it out of the park. Instead of focusing on getting the callback, I was focusing on getting the part. What I should have done was focus on getting the callback. Then, once I had the callback, work on getting the second callback. Then, once I had the second callback, work to get the producer's meeting. Once I had the producer's meeting, work to get the screen test, and so on. I want you to do the same thing with your direct outreach. Take it one step at a time and you'll do fine, and it will feel more authentic to you.

Finally, make sure that your suggested next steps are very clear. You must let the reader know exactly how to take advantage of your offer, what you want him to do, and when you want him to do it.

Before you send out any direct outreach letters or e-mail, ask yourself the following questions:

- Is the letter personalized?
- Am I being direct without pushing?
- Do I connect with the reader about one of his accomplishments?
- Did I indicate that I will follow up?
- Do I know how I'm going to follow up?
- Am I being real in the letter?
- Am I clear about the next steps and how he can contact me?
- Do I know—and have I articulated—what's in it for him?

3.10.1 Written Exercise: Identify three people you'd like to reach out to directly and personally. (These may be prospective clients, decision makers at an organization or association, or the press.)

3.10.2 Written Exercise: Choose one of the people you identified and write your own direct outreach letter using the guidelines above. Remember to ask yourself the direct outreach letter-writing questions before you send the letter.

3.10.3 Booked Solid Action Step: Send the letter you've just written. Decide how you'll follow up and when, and schedule in your calendar the time to do so.

Calls

I've had clients tell me they'd rather dig ditches than call someone on the phone that they don't know and attempt to make an offer. I've also had clients tell me they have no problem and actually enjoy calling people they don't know. Personally, I'm in the first group. I will certainly call someone I don't know to talk about a cross-promotion opportunity or another business development initiative like booking a speaking gig or submitting an article, but I would never cold call someone who did not know me or my company and offer him my coaching and consulting services.

As previously discussed, you want to keep in touch and follow up with every ideal client or potential customer you meet. How you do that will be your choice, but the good-old-fashioned phone is not to be underestimated for making real, personal, and emotional connections with potential clients and business contacts.

Following up using the phone is very different from cold calling someone because you have permission to do so. Also, because e-mail has become our main form of business communication, so few people actually use the phone that it's quite a lovely surprise to hear someone's voice and really get to know him by having a meaningful conversation.

When you make that call, be brief, direct, and straightforward. Be very clear and concise with your communication. Speak confidently and with a full voice.

> **3.10.4 Booked Solid Action Step:** Choose one of the people you identified earlier and give that person a call. If you'd like, you can call the same person you wrote the letter to, as a way of following up.

E-Mail

E-mail is an amazing tool. You can connect with anyone around the globe almost instantaneously. When you meet someone at a networking event or at a social occasion, or you are personally referred to someone, sending a quick and personal e-mail is an effective way of ensuring that you continue to deepen the connection. But e-mail can also be the easy way out because it can be impersonal. In addition, most spam arrives in the form of an e-mail, so e-mail is very easy to ignore and typically doesn't make a profound impression. When's the last time you heard someone exclaim, "Wow! I just got an e-mail, can you believe it?!"

The moral of the story is to use e-mail in conjunction with the other direct outreach tools. Think of it as a way to bridge each one of the outreach tools we're discussing.

Postcards

Postcards are a great direct outreach tool. In fact, postcards are the staple of the direct mail industry. You probably got a couple in the mail this week. Postcards can quickly encourage people to take action on something direct and simple like going to your web site, calling a number, or tuning in to a television program. They work best when the action required is free and easy and when you're giving away something of value.

Don't you think it would be nice if you got a personalized, branded postcard from someone just a few days after you met him? How often does that happen?

3.10.5 Booked Solid Action Step: Purchase a dozen or more postcards and the appropriate postage. Keep them with you in your planner, briefcase, purse, or car, and the next time you meet someone you'd like to follow up with, immediately jot down a short personalized message and drop it in the mail. She'll be impressed that you took this extra effort and will remember you for it. Or better yet, visit www.1800Postcards.com to order personalized postcards that are remarkably inexpensive.

Brochures and Flyers

If your business is new, you may want to skip creating brochures and flyers. Your business is going to be changing so quickly in your first few years that spending a considerable amount of money designing and printing brochures and flyers just does not add up.

I know, you could design them yourself and print them on your personal printer. *Please don't*—not unless you're a talented designer with experience. Don't you want materials that represent you and your work to be brilliantly designed and highly sophisticated? Most brochures and flyers that I see professional service providers using are just plain horrible. They're usually designed using a Microsoft® Publisher or Word template, printed on regular thin copy paper, and filled with clichés and bland copywriting that doesn't even remotely speak to the talent and professionalism of the brochure's owner.

I believe you can wait on brochures until you've found that the way you talk about what you do, your offers, your prices, and so on have been holding strong for at least a year. If you are going to create flyers yourself, just make them very simple, clean, and information-based.

Whatever-It-Takes Direct Outreach

You can do a lot to grab attention, but attention is only valuable if it shows you off in a light that's flattering. If you're a creative soul with a strong and developed sense of play, you'll have a lot of fun conceiving of and executing no-rules attention-grabbing direct outreach campaigns.

Years ago when I worked in the corporate world, I had a boss who swore, literally, every which way 'till Sunday that I had to get an executive at a big cosmetics firm to agree to sponsor one of our programs. The only problem was that the executive wouldn't take my calls. I tried to explain to my boss that I didn't think they were the right fit for us, but he disagreed and directed me to make it happen.

After a few more weeks of trying to get a meeting with the executive, I was about to give up when his assistant, the toughest gatekeeper I'd ever encountered, let slip that he was out to lunch when I called. Just making pleasant conversation, I asked, "Oh, yeah? What'd he go for today?" "Chinese, it's his favorite . . ." she replied, without thinking much about it. "Okay, thanks. Have a nice day!" I said and hung up.

The next day I had a great big order of Chinese food delivered to him personally. Inside the order was the proposal for the project. Twenty minutes after the food arrived, I called him. This time I was put right through. I said, "Will you take a look at my proposal now?" "No," he answered. "Why not?" I asked. "Because I don't like any of the dishes you sent over." "What do you like?" I asked. He told me. I said, "If I send these over tomorrow, will you read my proposal and take a meeting with me?" He said, "No, but I will read your proposal. If I like it, then I'll take a meeting with you." I said, "Great. When would you like me to follow up?" He told me and we said goodbye. He did like the proposal and subsequently took a meeting with me. We never actually did a deal. Turns out our companies weren't a good fit. But we became friendly, and he introduced me to one of my first clients after I left the corporate world and started my own business. You just never know.

One of my clients was trying to connect with a meeting planner at a large multinational corporation and couldn't get the planner to give him the time of day. After all his other direct outreach attempts failed, he sent her a coconut with a note that said, "You're a tough nut to crack. How about it?" She was still laughing when she called him to schedule an appointment.

Think creatively about what kind of fun, outrageous, no-rules attention-grabbing direct outreach strategies would work for you. Really let loose and let the ideas flow freely.

3.10.6 Written Exercise: List five wild, wacky, and unique ways to make a personal connection, especially with anyone you've been unsuccessful connecting with in the more traditional ways.

Promoting Through the Press

Publicity—promoting through the press—is free advertising, which we love. Typical examples include feature stories and product or service announcements published in either print or broadcast media. Publicity is especially effective as a promotional tool because people give more credibility to what they read or hear when it comes from news sources, whereas their belief in advertising messages is understandably often tainted with varying degrees of suspicion, which is why I rarely recommend that service professionals buy ads.

There are many outlets for stories, ranging from the local weekly and regional daily papers (important in keeping the local community informed about what's going on in their areas) to national newspapers, and an ever-increasing number of special interest magazines, television, and radio programs.

You can hire a PR firm on retainer in hopes that they will work very hard for you and get you lots of coverage that drives oodles of new referrals your way or you can do it yourself. Unless you have a very large amount of disposable income to put back into your business, I recommend that you be your own PR agent. The do-it-yourself PR resources I recommend are www.rtir.com, www.PRweb.com, and www.bacons.com.

- Look at www.rtir.com (Radio TV Interview and Report). It is widely read by radio show producers. You post an ad with your picture, your topic, your talking points, and your contact information, and if you're compelling, timely, and relevant, you'll get calls from radio hosts and producers to be a guest on their shows.

- Try www.PRweb.com; from what I can tell, this is the only service on the Internet that provides free global news distribution services—meaning that they really do provide free press release distribution to editors all over the world. You post your press release with them, and their service sends individual, permission-based e-mails to the editors who fit the appropriate profile for your press release.

- You may also want to consider going to www.Bacons.com and purchasing the media contact list that applies to your services, marketplace, demographics, and the geographic territory of your target audience. Bacons has it all: print, radio, and TV. For a small fee they will send your press material to the media list you specify.

As with all marketing, it may take a number of attempts to make a connection with an editor, producer, or writer, even at your local paper or radio station. However, the energy, time, and money you spend on promoting through the press can really jump start your business. Here are six simple steps that will help you work your own public relations campaigns:

The Six Steps to Planning and Executing Your PR Campaign

1. *Clarify your goals.* What are you trying to achieve? Are you hoping to attract exposure for a new program, an extraordinary success that your client has had, or the release of a new product?

2. *Identify whom you want to reach and connect with.* Not the people in the press, mind you; that will come soon. First identify whom you're trying to get your message to, your target market. Who are they, where do they live, what do they do, where do they shop?

3. *Choose which media outlets you're going to target.* Do this by identifying which publications your target market reads, what radio programs they listen to, what television programs they watch, and what associations they belong to. Then compile a list from most important to least important.

4. *Write the press release that makes your announcement.* You may also choose to have an expert write the release for you, while you do the submissions.

5. *Prepare for interviews.* Use note cards or paper to list your main points and the top five benefits of using your service, product, or program. This will help you organize your thoughts when you are called for an interview.

6. *Submit your press release by fax and e-mail to your list of media outlets.* Wait five business days and then call the recipients of your press release. Have your note cards at hand so you can interest the contact in what you've got to offer. If you don't make contact, leave a voice mail message. Just make sure you follow up.

You can easily input your own information into a sample press release and begin sending it out immediately. Go to the Free Resources section of www.BookYourselfSolid.com.

3.10.7 Written Exercise: List five media outlets that you're going to reach out to. Remember, they must serve your target market.

3.10.8 Written Exercise: Using the press release template you downloaded from www.BookYourselfSolid.com, write your own press release about an extraordinary result that one of your clients received from your services. This will be a great first step, and you'll have the press release ready to go except for a few minor adjustments.

Direct Outreach Plan

There are many ways to connect with potential clients and customers, but none of the tools I laid out are effective without a plan. After you identify a person or organization you'd like to reach out to, what do you do? Do you create a plan and then execute the plan? No? Well, that's okay because now you will and you'll be delighted with the success your new plan will bring.

1. Identify the individual you're going to reach out to.
2. Choose the steps you'll take to connect with her.
3. Create a schedule for your initiatives.
4. Execute the plan.
5. Evaluate it.

3.10.9 Written Exercise: For each of the three people you identified in Written Exercise 3.10.1, craft a direct outreach plan. Don't skip any of the above steps.

3.10.10 Booked Solid Action Step: Take the plan you've just created and schedule time to put it into action. Then follow through. All the thought and planning in the world won't mean anything if you don't take action and keep taking consistent action until you're booked solid.

Patience and Persistence Pay Off

It's important to understand that there is no *trick* to direct outreach. The magic formula to direct outreach, if there is one, is a consistent and open course of action throughout the life of your business. Direct outreach, like networking and keeping in touch, is something that must become a part of your regular routine. It takes time, but if you're patient and persistent, you *will* book yourself solid.

11

The Book Yourself Solid Referral Strategy

For it is in giving that we receive.

—Saint Francis of Assisi

Imagine enjoying deeper relationships with every client you work with while attracting three or four times as many wonderful new clients as you have right now. It's not only possible but simple and inexpensive. The key lies in generating client referrals. By starting an organized referral program, you can immediately and effortlessly connect with an increasing number of potential new clients.

Because your clients enjoy and respect working with you, they will be eager to recommend your services and products to their friends and family. In fact, the vast majority of your new clients already come to you as a result of word-of-mouth referrals, either directly or indirectly. If I had to guess, I'd guess that you don't have a program in place to benefit from all the word-of-mouth promotion that you could be receiving.

It is simple to increase your referral quotient exponentially. How many referrals do you get without a referral system right now? Now triple or quadruple that number. Potentially, that is the increase in clients you could be working with within the next month. Referral-generated clients are often more loyal, consistent, and better-suited to you than any other category of potential clients you could find.

Quick Referral Analysis

Let's look at how you've already received referrals. By identifying a situation in the past where a client or colleague, or someone else altogether, referred a client to you, you will recognize patterns that will help you consistently produce the results you desire.

3.11.1 Written Exercise: Start by remembering the last time a quality referral came to you:

1. From whom did the referral come?
2. What was the referral for, specifically?
3. Did the referral need your services immediately?
4. How were you contacted—by the person making the referral or the potential client?
5. Had you educated the referrer about your services before he or she made the referral?
6. How did you accept the referral and follow up?
7. Is that new referral a continuing client today?

You may have already noticed some of your strengths in generating referrals, or perhaps parts of the process need a little of your attention. Either way, we're creating an easy and profitable process.

Finding Referral Opportunities

Referral opportunities are all around you, and most are slipping through your fingers right now because either you aren't noticing them or you aren't acting on them. Start by choosing one day of the week that you can focus on where and when you could be asking for referrals. Don't get nervous yet! You are simply increasing your awareness of potential referral opportunities. Pay close attention and mentally seek out every possible situation in which you could see yourself asking for referrals.

> **3.11.2 Written Exercise:** Using the Book Yourself Solid Finding Referral Opportunities Log, begin to track daily referral opportunities. For a free version of our ready-made Finding Referral Opportunities Log, go to www.BookYourselfSolid.com and click on Free Resources to download it.

Your objective in using an opportunities log is to focus on the details of your referral interactions. You can then start to recognize the unlimited opportunities for referrals and overcome any limiting feelings you may have about asking for referrals.

The Book Yourself Solid Finding Referral Opportunities Log will help you see what works and what doesn't work in the referral process. If you study these interactions, you can learn from them and adjust your behavior accordingly while significantly increasing your referral quotient. You're going to be pleasantly surprised at the plethora of untapped referral opportunities that are appearing before you every day.

Beginning the Referral Process

Are you ready to begin working with eager new clients who have heard about your expertise and seek the benefits you offer? Never forget how profitable and prosperous your business can be. How committed are you? Are you convinced that this is something you absolutely must do? Yes? Okay, let's continue, you unshakable, committed one, you!

Step 1: Identify Your Clients' Benefits

Keep their benefits in mind when you speak to your clients about referrals. These are the reasons they work with you and why they would want
others to do the same.

3.11.3 Written Exercise: Create a list of the benefits your clients will experience by working with you. Keep going until you've exhausted all the possible benefits.

Step 2: Identify Why Others Would Refer Clients to You

What are the emotional, social, and professional benefits that go along with
being someone who refers people in need to those who can help?

3.11.4 Written Exercise: Bring to mind your two best clients and list the
reasons they would want to refer their friends and family to you. Again,
think in terms of benefits. How do they feel after having referred their
friends and family?

Examples: They feel great helping their friends improve their business or
life in a specific way. They feel special having made a positive influence in
their friends' lives. They feel important and knowledgeable about something. They feel connected and accepted when they introduce friends and
business associates to a high-quality professional. They feel confident that
they are a valuable resource in their friends' lives and that they sent them to
someone who is qualified, committed, and well-liked.

Step 3: Identify the Types of Referrals You Seek

Remember your red velvet rope policy ideal clients with whom you do
your best work?

3.11.5 Written Exercise: Write down the types of people you want your clients, associates, friends, and family to refer to you. Your friends and family may have no idea whom to refer to you.

Examples: Family members, best friends, neighbors, acquaintances, work associates, small business owners, executives, people going through divorce or struggling financially.

Step 4: Identify the Places Where Your Referrers Meet Ideal Referrals

Your goal here is to help your clients and other acquaintances understand who in their lives will benefit most from your services and products and where they cross paths with these people. You are helping them get a clear picture of the people in their lives who must meet you and work with you. With these two things in mind—whom your referrals should be referring and where they will meet them—you have all you need to start on the referral path.

3.11.6 Written Exercise: Write down the places where your referrers would meet or connect with good referrals for you.

Examples: At the office, taking the kids to school, neighborhood events, sporting events, lunch appointments, after-work socializing, charity functions, the gym, political events.

Step 5: Clarify and Communicate How Your Referrers Make a Referral

Let's focus on how to help your referrers have a simple conversation with a potential referral who will effectively connect them to you and your offerings. You can't leave this to chance. Being able to articulate what you do in a way that makes you stand out from the crowd and truly connects you to the people you're meant to serve is not only necessary, it's essential for booking yourself solid.

3.11.7 Written Exercise: Write down how you'd like your referrers to refer their contacts to you. What do you want them to say? How do you want them to talk about what you do? What specific words and phrases do you want them to use? Do you want them to say that you are "the best"? Do you want them to mention that you recently received an award for outstanding community service? Get very specific. Think of yourself as a one-person PR firm. You decide how you want people to talk about you.

Step 6: Ask for Referrals

If you want to increase your referral quotient by 50 percent, the best strategy is to ask for referrals. This is the simplest part of the Book Yourself Solid Referral Strategy, as well as the most important. The previous and following exercises will help you ask effectively. Please make sure to complete these exercises thoughtfully.

You can start today to seek out opportunities for referral conversations. Here are a few excellent situations that naturally lead to a referral conversation:

- Your ideal client thanks you for a great session or work well done.
- Your ideal client asks you for more services.
- Your ideal client asks for clarification on a process or concept.
- Your ideal client describes a past problem that you helped fix or goal you helped him or her achieve.

And here are some obvious situations:

- Your ideal client mentions a friend or business associate who's been facing the same challenges your client has faced.
- Your ideal client mentions she is going to an industry conference for a few days (and you serve businesses or individuals within that industry).

Or you can create the opportunity for a referral conversation by:

- Thanking clients for their energy and enthusiasm during your session or project.
- Clarifying their goals or making a suggestion to work on their own.
- Asking clients how they are feeling about the work you're doing together or about past challenges.
- Complimenting clients on their progress—always!

You can create referral opportunities through a million other positive, affirming questions or statements. Once you get clients talking, ask them about the value they get from your sessions. Use this as an open door to have them talk about how your services could benefit other people or organizations they have relationships with.

Step 7: Facilitate the Referral Connection

Offer to meet, consult with, or advise anyone who is important to your clients. Let them know that you want to help educate their friends about the benefits of your services.

- Hand out a card or send an e-mail that clients will pass on to friends and family.
- Better yet, ask them to write down the names of these people and ask them how you should best get in touch with them (phone or e-mail address) and *you* do it.

I want you to take the burden of calling or sending the e-mail off of your referrer. If you don't, you can lose 50 percent of the referral opportunities you've been afforded. Why? Not because your referrer doesn't want to make the referral happen but because life gets in the way. People are busy and they can get distracted by other tasks on their plate. If *you* actually make the connection and do the follow-up, it's sure to happen.

The same is true any time you personally meet potential clients. They say they're going to call you, and even if they have the best of intentions, things come up that get in the way, and you don't get a call. So I suggest that when you meet someone you really connect with and who has expressed interest in your services, you call him.

3.11.8 Booked Solid Action Step: Craft a brief e-mail with a short paragraph or two about whom you help and how you help them. (A version of your Book Yourself Solid Dialogue in written form works well for this.) Send this e-mail to each of your clients and any appropriate friends, family, and colleagues, with the request that they respond to you with ideas for potential referrals. A personal note of thanks completes the action.

Step 8: Follow Up with Referrals and Referrers

Contact new referrals and introduce them to what you have to offer—in a meaningful, connected, and helpful way. This is where your always-have-something-to-invite-people-to offer comes into play. It gives you a really easy way to start a conversation with the potential client and extend a no-risk, no-barrier invitation that is compelling and attractive. All you have to do is make a generous invitation and you've started the Book Yourself Solid Sales Cycle.

When beginning a relationship with potential clients, consider the following:

- Hold private meetings or demonstrations to eliminate any fear or embarrassment they may have about trying something new.
- Learn about any past experience with your type of services or products that they may have had and, most important, what they hope to achieve.

- Tell them what to expect, how you work, and the benefits they will experience.
- Include administrative details too: what to have available, if anything. Help clients feel as comfortable and prepared as possible.
- Provide third-party articles and facts that support your analysis in describing benefits they will achieve.
- Invite clients to work with you, and remember the Book Yourself Solid Super Simple Selling System. Offer a specific date and time that suits their schedule.

Practice Your Referral Presentation

- Speak with lots of expression, get excited, and show the passion you have for the benefits your services can offer.
- Smile.
- Make eye contact.
- Be confident.
- Open your heart.
- When your potential client starts speaking, listen.

3.11.9 Booked Solid Action Step: Make the commitment to ask for referrals every day for five days straight.

Are you as excited as I am about the dozens of potential clients you're going to meet? Just think about all those potential clients who've been searching and waiting to be introduced to an expert like you. I hope and expect that you will serve your potential clients and community by immediately starting to ask for client referrals. Once you start speaking with your potential clients on a deep and personal level, they will see you as far more than just your title. They will see you with more value, dimension, and a higher level of respect.

This meaningful connection is the key to achieving a greater level of prosperity and personal satisfaction. It's the Book Yourself Solid way.

Who Wants What You Want?

While some of your clients may refer others to you without your having to ask, many won't. As I mentioned earlier, it isn't that they don't want to; they're just busy with their own lives and it hasn't occurred to them. While it may feel awkward at first to ask for referrals from your clients, give it a try. You'll be surprised at how willing they are to do so once you've brought it to mind. After all, they'll want their friends, family, and business associates to experience the same great benefits they have. And they'll enjoy being able to help you as well. When someone has a positive effect on one's life, even in small ways, it feels good to give something back, and referrals are a great way to do it.

Other Professionals—The Other Source of Referrals

Other professionals who offer services and products that are complementary to your own, and work with your target market, are ideal sources of referrals. When you operate from a perspective of abundance and cooperation, rather than from scarcity and competition, it becomes easy to reach out to others to develop relationships that can be mutually beneficial. The more you refer to others, the more they'll be inspired to refer to you.

Many service professionals have a formal referral group with five or six other professionals who serve the same target market but offer complementary services and products. By joining an organization like Business Network International or joining a referral-exchange group at BookYourselfSolid.com, you'll greatly extend your reach and build your reputation by having others talk about you and your services.

Think Big

Get creative! Talk to your barber or hair stylist, your real estate agent, anyone who comes into contact with a large number of people who could be potential clients for you. Don't forget to reach out to those with large on-line subscriber lists that serve your target market.

Whose newsletter do you subscribe to that has a subscriber list of thousands? Let them know about your services, products, and programs, and ask if they'd be willing to let their subscribers know what you're up to. But first, ask what you can do for them—what's in it for them.

Affiliate Fees and Rewards Programs

Create rewards for those who refer others to you. A reward could be any-thing from a formal affiliate program, where you pay cash for referrals, to coupons for discounts on your services, products, or programs, or a basket of gourmet food.

Some professionals worry about losing money by paying affiliate fees. The numbers tell a different story—that you'll *make* money by paying for referrals. Say you charge $500 per month for your services and you cur-rently have 10 regular clients. You're currently earning $5,000 a month. Now let's say that each one of your 10 clients refers one more client to you at $500 per month. That's another 10 clients for another $5,000 a month. If you give a referral fee of 10 percent, you'll be paying each referrer $50 per referral for a total of $500 in referral fees. Would you spend $500 to make $5,000 for a profit of $4,500 and a new monthly income of $9,500, almost double what you were making? I would. And think about what this means if you are currently making $40,000 or $50,000 per month.

Strike While the Iron Is Hot

Nurture the relationships you develop with those who refer others to you, and *always* follow up right away on any referrals you get. You'll then create not merely satisfied clients but raving fans by delivering your best work. Before you know it you'll be booked solid.

12

The Book Yourself Solid Web Strategy

The shortest distance between two points is under construction.
—Noelie Altito

If You're Not Online, You're Out of Line

You'd be hard pressed to show me a very successful service professional who doesn't have a web presence. It's a critical aspect of being able to start and continue conversations with potential clients. To carry on marketing conversations with potential clients, you must be able to follow up with the potential clients who come to you interested in your services or products. If you don't have a web site, you're missing out on the best and most efficient way to start these kinds of marketing conversations.

In this comprehensive chapter, I'll be walking you through the purpose and benefits of having a web site, the biggest mistake most people make online, web site content structure—including the 10 most effective formats for service professionals—what to look for in a web designer, the nine most important and easy-to-understand web site traffic generation strategies, and the five essential principles of web site visitor conversion.

And I promise to make it as easy to understand as a day at the beach—or at least a day at the beach with your laptop.

Before we get into the technical aspects of what makes a great web site, get out a pen and a piece of paper and write this down:

> *The effectiveness of my web site is directly proportional to how solution-oriented my offers are.*

Now post it in your office where you can see it as you're designing or redesigning your site. Your web site can be the single most effective tool for attracting and securing clients—if it's done right.

Purpose and Benefits of Having a Web Site

There are numerous purposes and benefits to having a web site and developing a strong web presence. Your own web site:

- *Positions you as an expert.* Perception is everything on the Internet. Having your own web site increases your visibility, credibility, and trustworthiness.
- *Builds your brand identity.* Your web site represents you and your business in the marketplace.
- *Reaches a global marketplace.* If you have a product available on your web site, you'll expand your geographic marketplace from your local neighborhood to the entire world.
- *Creates a 24×7 passive-revenue profit machine.* The Web never sleeps, which means that you can turn your computer and web site into a cash register around the clock, and many, if not all, of the processes can be automated.
- *Builds your database.* A web site can instantly increase the effectiveness of your sales cycle by building a targeted list of potential clients who have given you permission to follow up with them. A web site

with an opt-in allows you to provide value while building your database (by offering something of value in exchange for e-mail addresses). Remember, your visitors must see your offers and your services as opportunities worthy of their investment, even if that investment is as small as an e-mail address.

- *Allows for filtering out unsuitable clients.* All of your marketing materials can guide potential clients to your web site, where you save precious time by allowing them to familiarize themselves with you, your services, your procedures, and your prices before they contact you for more information. They can then determine whether they feel they'd be well-suited to work with you.

- *Provides an opportunity for bold self-expression and learning.* Your web site is a fantastic vehicle through which to express yourself. It is an extension and a representation of you and what you offer.

The Biggest Mistake Most People Make Online

If your web site does not convert a good percentage of the traffic that lands on your site, it's ineffective and may even be useless. *Convert* means that your visitors give you their e-mail addresses (usually in exchange for some sort of gift) along with permission for you to follow up on a regular basis, and *traffic* means visitors. So your goal is to convert your visitors into potential clients and then into current clients.

A pretty web site that does not successfully convert visitors into potential clients is pointless. Sure, you may get a few calls because someone visited your site, or sell a few products, but 99 percent of the people who visit your site will not come back again. It's not because they don't like what you have to offer, but people are busy and most don't even remember how they got to your site in the first place.

As a successful online marketer, you will focus on building what is called a *list* of potential and current customers and clients who eagerly anticipate your messages and offerings. Remember how important building trust over time is. If your primary objective is to offer extraordinary value up front in exchange for an e-mail address and permission to follow up, then you can make relevant and proportionate monetized offerings later on, once you've built trust.

Content and Structure

The content and structure of your web site include the information you wish to convey and how you organize and label it for easy navigation. Just as you can leverage the same content for an information product into several different formats, you can choose a variety of formats to lay out your web site content.

As you consider your content and structure, your focus should be on your target market. It is especially critical when you're working with a designer to be an advocate for your target audience. Your designer may not care who your target audience is, but you must.

Your content and structure are the key elements in determining whether your web site is effective. The content has to be relevant to your target market and the layout should make it obvious where the visitor needs to go and what the visitor needs to do.

Visitors to your site want information and resources that will assist them in their work and their lives. If they can't find what they need, they'll get frustrated with your site and with you. The result is a lost connection. Strive to make your site easy to navigate and you'll establish considerable rapport with your visitors because they will feel that you already know and understand them.

3.12.1 Written Exercise: What is the primary objective of your web site? (Hint: I answered this question for you earlier.)

Web Site Basics

We're going to focus on the homepage format of your web site because it's the most important real estate on your site. Industry studies suggest that you have only three seconds to create a connection with a new visitor to your site or they move on.

Make sure your homepage includes these basics:

- *Choose a client-centric and easy to remember web site name.* Were you aware that you can have more than one domain name that will direct potential clients to a single site? You can with domain forwarding or pointing, and you should. I urge you to have a minimum of two domain names—one being your name, the most likely thing that a client will try if they don't have your web address handy—www.MichaelPort.com—and the other being something that speaks to the market you serve: www.SmallBusinessExcellence.com. They both go to the exact same site.
- *Speak to your target market.* Your site should speak to the needs and desires of your target market. This is where you offer solutions and describe the benefits of those solutions.
- *Declare your call to action.* You must have a clear call to action that is easy and obvious for your potential clients to find.

The Ten Most Effective Web Site Homepage Formats for Service Professionals

1. The Brochure

A brochure web site is usually about five pages and is the online equivalent of a written brochure. It's the most common format of web site for the service professional. Generally a brochure web site includes information about you and your company, your services, and some resources, for starters.

The risk you take when using this format is that it can appear to be all about you rather than the people you serve, and if you aren't creative, your web site may not look much different from another service professional's web site.

One way to increase the effectiveness of a brochure web site is to combine it with another one of the other homepage formats I suggest.

The conversion rates (the percentage of visitors who are opting-in to your newsletter or buying a product or service) will likely be higher with most of the homepage formats I suggest below. A good example of this is www.BookYourselfSolid.com.

2. The E-mail Converter

The e-mail converter format—aka the squeeze page—is the ultimate one-step web site. There's only one thing to do on an e-mail converter web-page—give your e-mail address in exchange for something of value, like a special report or whitepaper, minicourse or coupon, or access to your al-ways-have-something-to-invite-people-to offer. You must have a very compelling offer right out front that prompts visitors to engage because you've got only one shot at getting that all-important e-mail address.

The e-mail converter format can easily be combined with many of the other formats. For example, take a look at www.MarketingWith Postcards.com.

You will need a tool that allows you to capture e-mails and automati-cally send customers a confirmation and follow-up. The best system on the market for this, and one that I personally endorse, is www.Booked SolidCart.com.

3. The One-Page Sales Letter

A one-page sales letter is designed specifically to encourage buying a prod-uct, program, or service. You may have come across one-page sales letters that you found hyped-up, over-the-top, and all about the hard-sell. That's not who you are, so your one-page sales letter won't come off that way. Remember, all of your marketing must be designed to speak to your target market. If your target market responds to hyped-up, over-the-top, and hard-sell marketing messages, well then, that's what you'll use. I have a feel-ing that's not the case. The reason so many online marketers use the long-form one-page sales letter is that when it's done well, it's a good tool for selling products. It is designed to elicit a direct response from the reader. Long-form one-page sales letters work well because they're not really meant to be read in their entirety. They're designed to be scanned. That's why they often boast big colorful headlines and bullets and bold text and highlighted text, for example. The important point here is this: Know your market. A good example of a one-page sales letter can be found at www.TrafficSchool System.com. The Traffic School is a coaching program that I co-created to help you generate more web site visitors and increase sales.

Again, you will need a tool like www.BookedSolidCart.com that enables you to sell your products and services online: Set up order pages, take credit cards, and automatically send customers an e-mail confirmation.

4. The Menu of Services

A menu of services is a homepage that offers a list of scenarios that you provide services for. Your visitors will choose one of the scenarios based on their needs and then they're automatically taken to a more targeted message on another page. Then you can start a virtual conversation through the more targeted page that speaks specifically to them and their situation and how you can help. It allows you to provide customized value and a level of interaction lacking in other formats.

But beware: Using this format puts you at risk for appearing to do too many things rather than serving as an expert in a single area. It's also a less direct line to an opt-in that begins a conversation because they're required to choose another page first.

5. The Assessment

Offering an assessment that speaks directly to the urgent needs and compelling desires of your web site visitors (your target market) is a wonderful way to create immediate connection and help your potential clients assess how much they actually need your services. Assessments can be created in the form of a quiz, survey, or personal profile. They're effective because they're interactive, they engage the client, and they invite a qualifying action; to receive answers to the assessment would require the assessment takers to enter their e-mail address. The entire process can be automated, and you can create new assessments or quizzes to have on your web site to draw repeat visitors back to your site.

For a great example of a site that uses the assessment as a homepage, check out www.eDiets.com.

6. The Testimonial

One of the most effective ways to create awareness for the valuable services you offer is to have other people talk about you and what you do. The testimonial homepage format is designed with this purpose in mind. You gather together all of the rave reviews you've received and place them on the homepage of your web site. Your testimonials should speak to the results that your clients have received by working with you.

Visitors to your site want to hear what you have to say, and they'll be influenced even more by the high praise of others. In fact, audio and video testimonials can be even more effective than written ones.

If you're interested in putting audio and video on your site, take a look at www.AudioTestimonialsOnline.com. They have an amazing feature that allows your customers to call a toll-free number and record their audio testimonial over the phone. You then click a couple of buttons, put the audio on your site, and you're done! You can also do something similar with video using their product.

7. The Portal

Typically a portal site offers a catalog of web sites, a search engine, large amounts of content about certain subject matter, or all of the above.

It's not often used for the service professional but can be a good choice for you if you have many products, services, and programs that are different from each other or serve different target markets. This format allows you to present your multiple offerings so that visitors can choose which product or service they want to learn more about based on their needs. However, you have to make sure that you don't create a homepage that offers too many choices that may potentially confuse your visitors.

I use this format for my homepage at www.MichaelPort.com. In fact, it's really the only page at www.MichaelPort.com. From there my visitors can access all my web sites.

8. The Content Generator

The content generator is a great way to capture e-mail, to start to identify exactly what your target market needs and wants, to generate content for your product or service, or to find out what people want in a seminar or other type of event you may be offering. It's highly interactive and encourages conversation. Through a content generator you can provide a personal response, giving the visitor an opportunity to ask a question or give an opinion, which you can then compile for use in marketing at a later date, while at the same time responding to start a conversation.

9. The Viral Entertainment Site

Viral entertainment sites are based on the buzz marketing approach—getting other people to spread your messages. A viral entertainment site offers some sort of media that is either emotional, funny, or makes people say "Wow!" It's a great way to make a positive connection with lots of people who don't even know you. Take a look at www.TheTimeMovie.com.

10. The Blog

What is the blog homepage format? Here's how Andy Wibbels, author of *Blogwild!* describes a *blog*:

> A blog—short for "weblog"—is often described as an online diary. The most recent entries (called posts) appear on the homepage of the blog with links to archives of older posts. Archives are organized by date and often categorized by topic. Many times each post has a form for readers to add their own comments at the end to give their opinion or reaction to the post's content.
>
> The real genius in blogs appears in the process of how they are written. You can update your blog instantly from any Internet connection on any computer anywhere in the world. It's super easy. If you can send an e-mail, you can publish a weblog.

The biggest drawback to a blog is that it works only if you post to it regularly. If it doesn't change often, that's worse than having a static regular web site. For an example of an excellent blog, go to www.Andy Wibbels.com.

What Works For You?

3.12.2 Written Exercise: Go online and find three or four web sites you like and three or four that you dislike. List the formats they use and the features you like and dislike, and why. These will be useful as examples of what you want—and don't want—to show your designer. If possible, choose web sites for this exercise that provide services to your target market and note what they're offering and how they present their offering. This will give you a sense of what's already out there and may spark new ideas.

What to Look for in a Web Designer

When I started my solo-business, I spent over $6,000 on a web site with lots of funky animation that I never used—or I should say, I used it for five months to no avail. The site may have looked cool, but it wasn't effective. I learned pretty quickly to look for a web designer who is proficient in all three of the critical skills of web design: design, marketing, and programming. I encourage you to do the same. You can find designers I personally recommend at www.BookYourselfSolid.com.

Nine Book Yourself Solid Web Traffic Strategies

If you plan on successfully using your web site to help you get clients, you need to learn how to create a steady flow of traffic to your site. That's called *generating traffic*. These are the nine most important and easy-to-understand tried-and-true techniques and strategies for generating more traffic to your site.

1. Get Listed in Search Engines and Optimize Your Site

Search engine optimization is all about how to get the search engines to notice your site and, ideally, to give you a good ranking. Then when someone searches for what you're offering, your listing will be displayed in a high position.

To get listed with most of these search engines, they must know you exist. So the first thing to do is submit your site to each search engine. Many search engines offer you the option of paying a fee to have your submission expedited. This does not imply that you'll get a better ranking, just that they'll *spider* (a program that automatically fetches webpages) your site sooner than they would without the additional fee.

Once you've submitted your site for inclusion in the major search engines, make sure your site is optimized with the best keywords, that is, words or phrases that your target market types into the search engine to find what you provide. Because every search engine has different criteria for ranking web sites, and none of them actually want you to know what these criteria are, the most effective strategy for search engine optimization (SEO) is to build content-rich pages that your visitors want to see, pages that are legitimately filled with the same keywords and phrases they use to search for what you are offering.

How do you determine what keywords and phrases will help you drive the most traffic? You focus on the urgent needs and compelling desires of your target market. What would a potential client type into a search engine to find what they're looking for? It may not be what you think. The best keywords and phrases are the emotional, benefit-filled terms that:

- Have the most number of searches.
- Have the least amount of competition.
- Draw targeted traffic that is ready, willing, and able to invest in your services.

In fact, there are a number of tools that tell you exactly how many people are searching on your chosen keywords and phrases. Google offers a free keyword search tool at www.adwords.google.com/select/Keyword Sandbox. Overture offers a free keyword search tool at http://inventory .overture.com/d/searchinventory/suggestion.

When you find the right keywords and phrases for your site, optimize your site using these same words and phrases. Understanding your best keywords is essential for the success of all your online marketing.

3.12.3 Written Exercise: Identify the top five keywords and phrases for your site.

3.12.4 Booked Solid Action Step: Now that you have your keywords and phrases, take these seven actions and begin to optimize your site, or better yet, hire someone to do it for you:

1. Create a unique title for every page on your site with the keywords for that page in the title—the title should describe the benefits you provide.
2. Make sure your web designer is using the <h1> and <h2> tags on your webpages and including your keywords and phrases in them. Search engines consider these tags to contain the most important content descriptions of what is on the page.
3. Put your keywords in the text that is linked to subpages on your site.
4. Use your keywords and phrases in the copy text of your site—even bold them in a few places, but don't go crazy.
5. Include your keywords at the top and bottom of your pages, but again, don't go crazy.
6. Tell your web designer to include your keywords in the ALT attribute of your <IMG> tag.
7. Tell your web designer to include your keywords in the TITLE attribute of your <A> tag.

Here are a few things to make sure you don't do, no matter what anyone tells you:

- Don't ever try to trick the search engines. That is not the Book Yourself Solid way, and you'll get blacklisted from the search engines if they think you're trying to trick them. No one, not even a search engine (maybe especially a search engine), likes to be fooled.
- Along these same lines, do not try to hide your keywords or stuff your page with keywords by repeating them over and over again.
- Don't use frames or lots of flash animation. Neither are search-engine friendly.

Remember, search engines have a job to do for their customers—to bring up results of great content that will match their search terms. Make their job as easy as possible.

2. Boost Your Link Popularity

Boosting your link popularity (the number of inbound links) and having quality inbound links (links from sites that have a good ranking and serve the same target market as you or offer related content) pointing to your web site will help you in two ways:

1. It improves your search engine ranking.
2. It provides a way for more quality traffic to find your site.

Please don't even think about fooling around with link exchange software or programs. Boosting your link popularity has to be done legitimately.

It's important to know that you need to create relationships with other links that already have good web traffic and status. Exchanging links with five of your friends—who just built their web sites—is a good and enterprising idea, but it's not going to do much for your search engine ranking and probably won't help drive any significant traffic to your site. If you don't know many other people who have a strong web presence, here's what you can do:

1. Put together a list of other professionals who serve the same target market and have already created some demand for their services and products.
2. Go to www.Yahoo.com and enter this text: linkdomain:URL.com.
3. Click the search button and you'll get a listing of all the sites on Yahoo that are linked to the URL you entered. You can then contact those sites, make friends, add value to their life and work, and offer to trade links with them.

3.12.5 Written Exercise: Identify five sites that have a decent Google ranking and serve the same target market as you serve. To see the PageRank of a site, you need to download and install the Google toolbar from www.Google.com. When you get to the Google homepage, click on the link that says "more."

3.12.6 Booked Solid Action Step: Now reach out to the owner or web-master of each site, make friends, add value to their life and work, and offer to trade links with them. Make sure that you link to them first so they can see that you're intent on serving them.

3. Leverage Your E-mail Signature

One of the most often overlooked methods of promoting your services is through your e-mail signature file. This is the information that you put at the close of your e-mail. It's a simple and effective way to tell people about what you have to offer and to encourage them to sign up for your newsletter or any other no-barrier-for-entry offer that you make.

You could consider asking a question in your signature file and include a link to your site where the answer to the question will be waiting. Here's an example:

Are you booked solid with high-paying clients all day tomorrow?
No? Then go to www.BookYourselfSolid.com.

Or keep it short and simple with something like this:

How to Get More Clients Fast
www.BookYourselfSolid.com

You could also include an autoresponder e-mail address that will automat-ically send out an article or special report that gives the answers, using a system like www.BookedSolidCart.com. When you deliver the article or special report as promised, you can also ask the recipients if they want to subscribe to your newsletter for more valuable resources or tips. For exam-ple, here's how my offer would look:

Want more clients now? Send e-mail to newsletter@bookyourself solid.com for a free subscription to my monthly newsletter on how to attract more clients quickly and easily.

> **3.12.7 Booked Solid Action Step:** Create a compelling e-mail signature and begin using it immediately.

4. Promote Your Site Using Article Directories

One of the best methods for building your credibility and driving traffic to your web site is by writing informative articles on topics that are close to your heart and submitting them to niche web sites and article directories for free.

Why does this work? Web surfers, just like search engines, gobble up information, which means the people who manage web sites are desperate for good content to feed them. They understand that people recognize a web site as a valuable resource if there is adequate, timely, and frequently updated content to peruse. If the site owners provide quality information not found anywhere else, people will regularly return to their pages to acquire it.

If you're supplying this content, you can catapult your name into the limelight and become known as a category authority. As long as your written information meets the specific needs of these niche web sites and article directories by being relevant, timely, and well-written, most editors will be happy to accept your article and post it on their site.

You may be wondering: "How does that generate traffic to my web site?" I'm glad you asked. By including a brief byline about yourself at the end of your article, with a link to your site, you can generate qualified traffic back to your web site pages. Since readers have already been introduced to your expertise and credible advice, they'll be interested in reading more of your worthy material and learning about your offerings.

The beautiful part about writing articles to share across the Web is that there is no barrier for entry whatsoever. Posting your articles on these niche web sites and in article directories gets your name and web site address in front of untold numbers of viewers. As a bonus, your article appears in search results displayed by engines like Google, MSN, and Yahoo.

In Chapter 14, we continue to discuss how to promote your web site and yourself by writing articles.

5. Participate in Discussion Boards and Listserve Groups

A discussion board is a general term for an online bulletin board where you can leave messages with questions or comments and expect to have other members of the discussion board respond to your messages. A list-serve group is similar except that all communication takes place by e-mail rather than on an online board.

3.12.8 Booked Solid Action Step: Find the most active online discussion boards and listserve groups that serve your target market and are focused on topics you know a lot about. As a member of the group, you can make intelligent, thoughtful posts that add value to the discussion topic. You might answer other members' questions or you might suggest helpful re-sources or simply provide your opinions on issues that relate to your indus-try. And you never know—you may learn a lot by reading what others have to say.

To find discussion boards and listserve groups for your needs, visit Google groups at www.google.com/groups and Yahoo groups at http://groups.yahoo.com.

6. Cross-Promote through Marketing Partners

This is one of my absolute favorite online marketing strategies because it allows me to partner with, and promote, other people whom I think are fabulous while they do the same for me. We've talked about how impor-tant it is to get other people to talk about you in order to quickly build trust with new potential clients. Well, cross-promoting through marketing partners is the best way to do so.

If my friend and colleague, Andrea J. Lee of www.AndreaJLee.com, sends out an e-mail to her newsletter subscribers endorsing my services, products, or programs, her subscribers are more likely to trust me. When I promote her, the same will be true. It makes it much easier to build relationships with potential clients that way. It's just like meeting a great friend of a great friend of yours. You love your friend and if your friend loves that person, you assume that person is great. The same goes for cross-promoting online (and offline).

You can cross-promote like this on many levels: between you and another service professional who happens to serve the same target market or with larger associations and organizations. If you're an accountant who serves small business owners and you develop a relationship with the membership director for an online small business association that has 75,000 members and she promotes your services to their membership, just think about all of the newsletter signups you're going to get. And just think about all of these new potential clients who turn into clients. The possibilities are limitless. That is why this is my favorite online marketing strategy.

Here are some other strategies to consider:

- Co-produce special promotions you could not afford on your own.
- Have a contest with the prizes contributed by your partners. For the next contest, roles change, and you contribute your product or service as a prize for a partner's contest.
- Give customers a free product or service from a participating partner when they buy something that month from all of the partners listed on a promotional piece.

Online cross-promotion has the potential for a big marketing payoff because partners can successfully expand through each other's client base. Both you and your marketing partners can gain an inexpensive and credible introduction to more potential clients more effectively than with the traditional lone-wolf methods of networking, advertising, or public relations.

3.12.9 Written Exercise: Come up with several of your own unique ideas for cross-promotions and identify who might be a good marketing partner.

3.12.10 Booked Solid Action Step: Reach out, connect with, and share your ideas with the people you identified in Written Exercise 3.12.9.

---

7. Use Tell-a-Friend Forms

It's safe to say that a significant percentage of your clients will come from referrals. If your current raving fans are telling others about you offline, don't you think they would like to tell others about you online as well? Well, they can with a tell-a-friend form. Imagine that a visitor to your site likes what she sees and believes she has a friend who could benefit from your services. With a click on your tell-a-friend link, she can refer your site to her friend.

You'll need a script that can generate this form for you; www.BookedSolidCart.com offers this feature as well. You can even customize it so that it automatically sends a personalized e-mail promoting your site and its web address. It's an amazingly simple and effective strategy. Again, you're getting others to talk about you and help build trust between you and a potential client. If you are adventurous and would like to code your own tell-a-friend forms, you can find free tell-a-friend scripts by searching online.

3.12.11 Booked Solid Action Step: Create, or hire someone to create, a tell-a-friend form and begin using it.

---

8. Take Advantage of Thank-You Pages

One of the most underused pieces of online real estate is the "thank-you" page. It's the page that you get after you opt-in to a newsletter or special report, or take an online assessment, or purchase a product. Usually, the thank-you page just says "Thanks," with a line that says something like, "We really appreciate your business."

You can take advantage of this prime real estate by offering some very useful information. You could make another offer. It's a great place for your tell-a-friend form. Think about it. If someone just signed up for your newsletter or purchased a product, all signs point to the fact that he likes you and thinks you have a lot to offer. Don't you think he'd be inclined to tell a friend about you at that point? You bet he would.

3.12.12 Booked Solid Action Step: Make the necessary changes to your thank-you pages so that you begin making the most of this valuable online real estate.

---

9. Profit from Pay-per-Click Advertising

Using pay-per-click ads on search engines can be an effective marketing tool. Pay-per-click means that you pay a fee for each person who clicks on the ad. You may be surprised to realize that this is the first time I've mentioned spending money on advertising. Until now our other online strategies haven't cost a dime. You should not be spending much, if any, money online to generate traffic. If you show up in the top eight regular search results for your keywords, you certainly don't need to pay for clicks. But if you're not in that top eight, this is a great way to get targeted exposure for a small investment with the potential for a big return.

Pay-per-click ads allow you to connect with prospective clients as they're searching for services or products like yours. You create an ad and choose keywords that, when entered into the search engine, will bring up your pay-per-click ad along with the regular search results. You pay only when someone clicks through to your site from the pay-per-click ad.

These pay-per-click ads are good for generating traffic to your site and great for testing what keywords and keyword phrases generate a lot

of traffic and what percentage of that traffic converts to potential customers and actual customers. When you sign up for Google Adwords
(www.google.com/ads) and Yahoo (http://searchmarketing.yahoo.com)
pay-per-click accounts, you'll receive a code to put on your web site
that will allow you to track this data.

The position of your ad (highest to lowest) is determined by your bid
price, the amount you're willing to pay for a click (the exception is with
Google, where your position is determined by a combination of your bid
price and your click-through rate). You really need to be on the first search
page for your pay-per-click ads to generate significant traffic. Of course
you can affect your position by modifying your bid. But don't worry—you
can cap the amount of your daily spending so you don't exceed your
mortgage payment in pay-per-click ads. The other great thing about being
in the top three positions on Google and Yahoo is that you're then syndi-
cated onto other sites and search engines all over the Internet.

Be careful: Make sure you're converting the traffic you pay for. Keep in
mind that a web site is useless if you can't secure the e-mail addresses of
visitors to your site and get their permission to follow up with them.
Nothing is worse than paying for traffic to your site and not converting
any of it. That's like driving a station wagon packed with cash and throw-
ing it out the windows as you aimlessly drive around town. However, if
you do convert a good percentage of that traffic to potential clients and a
percentage of them become clients, well, now you've invested wisely. In
fact, if you run the numbers, you can see your exact return on investment.

3.12.13 Booked Solid Action Step: Go to www.google.com/ads and set
up an account. Then create a test ad campaign for one of your products or
services. Make sure that you cap your daily spending at a low amount so
that you learn how to profit from pay-per-click before you rack up significant
fees. Google.com has great tutorials and help pages that can answer your
questions. Track your conversion so you know if you're getting a return on
your investment.

The Five Essential Principles of Visitor Conversion

You want to attract visitors to your web site and turn them into friends, then potential clients, and finally, current clients. You can generate all the traffic you want, but if that traffic does not give an opt-in request for more information, it's useless.

There are five essential principles of visitor conversion. Understand them, implement them, and profit from them, but never abuse them.

1. Enticement
2. Consumption
3. Endowment
4. Enhancement
5. Abandonment

Enticement

Your web site is like your home. What's the first thing you do when someone comes to visit? You offer him a drink and a bite to eat. You ask, "Are you hungry? Can I get you something to eat? How about a glass of water or some iced tea?" If you know your visitors well, you can offer them their *favorite* snack and beverage. In fact, when family or close friends come to visit, you make an extra trip to the supermarket to get all their favorites.

This is the principle of *enticement*. You offer something of value to your web site visitors as soon as they land on your site in exchange for their e-mail address and permission to follow up. They give it to you because they're interested in your enticement and they believe you'll deliver more good stuff in the days and months to come.

Be careful not to hide your enticing offers in the crevices of your web site. When you have a dinner party, do you hide the food around the house in strange places or set it just out of reach? Of course you don't. You put the hors d'oeuvres and munchies in the most obvious, accessible places possible. And sure enough, the places you put the hors d'oeuvres are exactly where everybody ends up hanging out! Have you ever been at a party where the host skimped on the hors d'oeuvres? Did you find that everybody started hanging around the kitchen as they got hungrier and hungrier? We're always searching for what we want and need, and your web site needs to speak to your visitors' needs and desires. So please, put your opt-in form in the most obvious place possible. I suggest you place it above the fold (the part of your homepage that is visible without having to scroll down).

As an experiment I recently surveyed the web sites of 50 random service professionals, and guess what? Only seven of them had a prominent opt-in form with something offering great and immediate value to their target market. The other 43 either did not have an opt-in form at all or did but put it in some obscure place that was hard to find. I hope that after publishing this book I can do another survey and see very different results.

3.12.14 Booked Solid Action Step: If you don't already have an e-course, special report, or other enticement to offer your visitors, create one using the easy steps I outlined in Chapter 7. Then ensure that you have an opt-in for your offer displayed prominently on your site.

Consumption

The principle of consumption follows the principle of enticement. It's something that I learned from a well-known Internet marketing expert named Alex Mandossian of www.TrafficConversionSecrets.com.

When your visitors have been enticed and have given you their e-mail address in exchange for a minicourse, white paper, special report, e-book, article, audio recording, coupon, or other free offer, you must follow up to help them consume the valuable information or experience they just received. Most people don't take advantage of all the opportunities available to them. It would probably be impossible to do so. An even smaller number of people follow up on all of the opportunities available to them through the Internet and e-mail, even the ones they've asked for. When someone does opt-in to receive your free offer, he may not really consume it—really use it, learn from it, and benefit from it. It's your responsibility to help him do so by following up with an e-mail.

Does it sound like it would be a lot of work? Oh, no, my big-thinking friend, it's not. You can use the automatic e-mail responder system from www.BookedSolidCart.com to set up a series of e-mail messages that are automatically sent to a new contact at any frequency you specify. You can send one a day, one a week, or one a month for a year—it's up to you. Your messages will check in with your new friend and begin to deliver the services you provide or other helpful resources.

The principle of consumption should follow the principle of enticement. It's just as you'd ask your guest, the one you generously supplied with her favorite snack and beverage, "How is the tea? Is it cold enough? Would you like more ice? Is it helping quench your thirst?" Maybe you'd offer a suggestion, "You know . . . if you squeeze the lemon like so, it tastes even better!" You'll ask your new friends how they're doing with the information you gave them and you'll help them consume it. If you do this well, you'll increase your likeability, and you'll create a more meaningful and lasting connection with your new friends, turning them from new friends into potential clients or maybe even into current clients.

3.12.15 Booked Solid Action Step: If you don't already have an autoresponder system to help potential clients consume your offer, set one up using www.BookedSolidCart.com, or hire someone to set one up for you.

Endowment

Endowment is one of my favorite principles for creating a powerful connection with a potential client, and it can be used online or off. The idea is to give or endow your services to qualified potential clients.

In Chapter 6, when discussing the always-have-something-to-invite-people-to offer, I mentioned that many service professionals offer complimentary consultations or other services as a strategy for building trust with potential clients. I also mentioned that I'm not a big fan of that. I don't like the idea of making yourself available to anyone and everyone whenever they want it. And how do you know the people booking your complimentary sessions are even qualified to work with you, let alone ideal clients? What kind of filtration system would you be using if you just gave free consultations to anyone who asked? It would be the kind that has a lot of holes in it. Instead, why don't you give gifts to very qualified people?

When visitors to one of my web sites sign up for a minicourse by e-mail or a special report or some other resource, I help them use the resource as the consumption principle dictates. But I then do something else based on the endowment principle.

About seven days after they sign up for the free resource, I send them a prewritten, preprogrammed e-mail automatically from www.BookedSolid Cart.com that offers them a free gift—a consultation with me or one of my certified coaches to help them with their most pressing business or marketing challenge. I call it a laser-coaching session. The coaching session is only 20 minutes, it's delivered over the phone, and it's scheduled by the visitor.

Does this sound like a lot of work to set up? Not at all. I use an online scheduling program called www.AppointmentQuest.com, where potential clients can schedule their sessions according to what is available on my online calendar.

There are a few rules, however. First, in order to qualify for the coaching session, all exercises in the previous parts of the free minicourse must be completed. I'm in the coaching and training business, so I want to make sure that the people my team and I work with are serious about their business. That unqualifies a whole bunch of people. Second, I gently note in my e-mails that they cannot be late or miss an appointment. If they do, they will not be able to reschedule. And finally, they have to send an e-mail to me one week before the scheduled sessions with the specific question or situation they want support and advice about. If a potential client is willing to adhere to these rules, I know I'm at least offering my time—and the time of my coaches—to someone who cares about her work and respects our time and energy as well. Never forget the red velvet rope policy of ideal clients.

More than 64 percent of the people who take advantage of these free laser-coaching sessions purchase my products, enroll in my coaching programs, or hire either me or one of my trained coaches for private coaching and consulting. I believe that many of the people who do not become clients directly after these complimentary sessions do talk positively about me and my company to their colleagues, which is just as important because there is no better marketing than the oh-so-sweet sound of people talking about the value you provide. They say, "He/she/they're the best! You've got to go to their web site."

At the end of the day, it just feels good to give to others who need your help. And as an added bonus, you'll also get really good at having sales conversations if you give lots of short consultations to qualified potential clients because at the end of the consultation, if you feel it's appropriate, you'll ask, "Would you like a partner to help you accomplish what we talked about today?"

3.12.16 Booked Solid Action Step: Decide what kind of endowment you'd like to set up and begin to implement it immediately. This type of marketing strategy is applicable to all service professionals.

Enhancement

Enhancement helps you sell more products or services or combinations of both. By the time someone has purchased a service from you, he has decided he trusts you and likes what you have to offer, and is willing to invest in the opportunity you're offering. It may also be a good time to suggest additional products or services that will enhance the service he's buying.

You see this principle at play for many consumer products. When you buy a computer, does the salesperson offer you just the computer or does she also offer you software to go on the computer, including virus protection, a firewall, and an external hard drive for backing up your data? Of course she does. She's well trained and knowledgeable about the product. She knows those are all things you need that will enhance the functionality of the product you're buying. In fact, many companies take this a step further and bundle all the products together for a better price than if you purchased each one individually.

What product or service can you offer at the point of purchase that will enhance *your* service? You might even offer someone else's product or service for an affiliate commission. For example, if you're a fitness professional and a new client is signing up for training sessions, are there products he needs or can use to help him achieve his fitness goals, like supplements, exercise equipment, or clothing? Be very careful when doing this so you don't push something on your new clients, especially something they don't need. If you really have something to offer that will enhance the service or product your clients are purchasing, offer it to them in good faith. Again, you can use a system like www.BookedSolidCart.com to do this automatically.

3.12.17 Written Exercise: Identify several possible enhancements you could be offering.

3.12.18 Booked Solid Action Step: Begin offering one of the enhancements you identified in the exercise above.

Abandonment

Our final traffic conversion principle is abandonment. It's fitting that abandonment is our final principle because it's about what happens when people leave your web site without buying something or opting-in to a free offer. You might think, "Well, that's it, they weren't interested in anything I had to offer and they left my site, what can I do?" There is a lot you can do.

It's time to turn to exit strategies that help you connect with visitors even when they're leaving your web site. Remember, the Book Yourself Solid way is all about asking, "How can I truly serve the people I'm meant to serve?" And talking to your web site visitors who are abandoning you about why they are leaving is one great way to do that.

Your web designer can create a webpage that opens automatically when visitors close your web site without opting-in to your list or purchasing a service or product. At first it might be a little surprising to your web visitors, but they'll probably be pleasantly surprised with what they see next: a picture of you, some text, and an audio message from you that automatically starts playing. You might say something like, "Thank you so much for visiting my web site. It means a lot to me that you took the time to learn more about how I can help you." You might then ask why they're leaving without signing up for your newsletter or downloading your free report or coupon for your services. Remember, your web designer can program this exit popup to open *only* if visitors did not opt-in or purchase a product. If they did, it won't open. You can let them know how your newsletter will help them or what they'll learn in the free report that you made available on your site. Basically, you're giving them a little extra encouragement that will increase the likelihood of them opting into your list.

If you need a tool to record your voice and put it on your web site, check out www.AudioTestimonialsOnline.com.

3.12.19 Booked Solid Action Step: Create an exit strategy and implement it, or hire someone to implement it for you.

Learning in Action

The Web is an extraordinary vehicle for self-expression. It offers huge opportunities for sharing who you are and what you offer as well as the privilege of connecting with others. There is a learning curve, but all great opportunities require that we learn something new. Two of the most important rules for doing big things in the world are learning in action and working with others.

Rule #1: Learn in Action

You must learn in real time and in action. You cannot afford to wait until everything is perfect to go out and do what you want to do. If you wait for perfection to go out in the world and do big things, you're never going to get there—or get anything done, for that matter. Many people hold themselves back because they think they have to know everything about how to do something before they actually do it. This is not true. You can and should learn while doing.

You cannot learn how to run or become a better runner without actually running. You can certainly read an article about how moving your arms in a particular way can help your stride, but until you put the tip into action, you won't really know or experience its truth. The same is true for Internet marketing or any other new skill you're interested in learning.

Rule #2: Work with Others

If you are completely uninterested in learning any new technology but still want to leverage the power of the Internet, hire or partner with others who have the skills, talents, and desires that you do not.

These days working solo does not mean working alone—far from it. I have a team I work with now that my business has grown beyond a one-person operation. But even in the beginning, I worked with *virtual assistants* who could do much of the work that I didn't like to do, and frankly, wasn't very good at. There are many virtual assistants who can help you with your Internet marketing. We offer these services at www.BookYourselfSolid.com. Come to the site and let us know what you need, and we'll be honored to serve you. As you embrace each of these marketing strategies, you will be pleasantly surprised at what you're able to accomplish in a very short time.

13

The Book Yourself Solid Speaking and Demonstrating Strategy

Write to be understood, speak to be heard, read to grow.
—Lawrence Clark Powell

Here's what the Book Yourself Solid Speaking and Demonstrating Strategy is *not*: You're in a cold hotel conference room crammed behind a skinny little table-desk slowly sipping a glass of ice water that is creating a condensation puddle at its base. You don't want to drink your water too fast because once it's gone, you won't have anything left to do. Not only that, your bladder feels like an overfilled balloon and the speaker, who's droning on about how great he is, has already gone 15 minutes over his scheduled time.

The Book Yourself Solid Speaking and Demonstrating Strategy can be used by virtually any service professional to get in front of potential ideal clients based on your knowledge, talents, and strengths. The wonderful thing about sharing your knowledge is that it's rewarding for both you and your audience. They will leave your presentation or event a little smarter, thinking bigger, and with an action plan that will help them implement what you've taught them. You will benefit because you'll know you've helped others, which is the reason you do what you do. And at the same time, you'll increase awareness for your services and products.

To get in front of your target market you can promote yourself or have others promote you. When you promote yourself, you're inviting your target market to something that is going to help them solve their problems and move them toward their compelling desires. When you are promoted by others, they put you in front of your target market. You may want to travel both routes. I do. Using the Book Yourself Solid Speaking and Demonstrating Strategy, I have been able to speak to over 20,000 service professionals over the last two years alone. You too can see these kinds of results using speaking and demonstrating to get your message out to the people you're meant to serve.

Self-Promotion

Of course, all of the Book Yourself Solid 7 Core Self-Promotion Strategies require that you promote yourself in one way or another. Even using the Book Yourself Solid Speaking and Demonstrating Strategy to get other people to put you in front of your target market requires that you promote yourself to the person who is going to give you that platform.

Let's look first at pure self-promotion, such as inviting your target market to events that you produce—not necessarily big workshops or conferences but simple, community-building, meaningful, enlightening events at which you can shine, show off your products and services, and build your reputation and credibility in your marketplace. These types of speaking and demonstrating events might fall into the category of an always-have-something-to-invite-people-to offer or you may charge admission. That will depend on where they fall into your slate of offerings. If you do use the always-have-something-to-invite-people-to offer in your marketing materials, when you meet potential clients or potential referral sources you'll just invite them to what you have to offer.

Conference Calls

Start a monthly or weekly call for clients to learn the benefits of working with you. Prepare a new, timely, and relevant topic every time. Pick up a magazine in your industry and use one of the articles to inspire your topic, invite guests to discuss their area of expertise, and ask your clients to tell you what they'd most like to hear about. The rest of the call will naturally flow into a Q&A session. Here are a few ideas to get you started and to spark your inspiration and creativity for your own unique ideas:

- Any service professional can offer a monthly or weekly Q&A on his or her area of expertise. No planning necessary—just show up and shine.
- Accountants can offer quarterly conference calls on updates on tax law along with planning strategies for decreasing tax liability, for example.
- Financial planners can offer conference calls on the best strategies for building wealth using the products they sell.
- Internet marketing consultants can offer conference calls or web conferences giving updates on search engine optimization and other web traffic generation strategies.
- Personal coaches can offer conference calls on their area of expertise: reducing anxiety, increasing focus, setting boundaries.

The conference line won't cost you a dime. You can go to www.Free Conference.com and get a free conference line for up to 100 people at a time. Then you record each call to your computer or digital recorder and upload it to your web site using www.AudioTestimonialsOnline.com. Those who couldn't make the actual call will still have the opportunity to listen to it and benefit from it. Archiving the calls on your web site is also a remarkable way of immediately establishing trust and credibility with new web visitors.

Demonstrations and Educational Events

These are similar to conference calls except they're conducted in person. Demonstrations and educational events are an excellent way to reach potential ideal clients if your services are physical or location-based or if the people you serve are all located in the same town or city. This is also a great alternative if you feel that a conference call doesn't speak to your strengths. This is another opportunity to get creative and express yourself. For example, you could create some excitement with an open house or outdoor demo at the park or at any other venue. Don't just invite your potential clients but also your current clients, friends, or colleagues who know the value of your services and are willing to talk about their experiences.

- Fitness professionals can offer a weekly physical challenge for clients and potential clients. Ask clients to bring a new friend every week. Each week a new type of workout would be planned with a social event afterwards.
- Real estate agents can offer weekly real estate investor tours where they fill a van or tour bus with active real estate investors and scour the neighborhood hotspots.
- Professional organizers can offer a monthly makeover where they go to a potential or new client's office or home, along with a small group of 10 or 15 people (it's not bad to have a waiting list for these types of offerings), and the professional organizer reorganizes the space and teaches the guests the basics of how to be more productive and effective through an organized office.
- A hair stylist can do something similar with the monthly makeover concept. She could even offer a contest or raffle each month, and the winner would get the makeover.
- Any service professional can host a no-cost or low-cost morning retreat. Be playful and adventurous. It doesn't have to be expensive, just creative. Allow clients to get to know you and meet other people with similar interests and goals. Make it as simple as serv-

ing tea, whole fresh fruit, and scones—and share your wealth of knowledge.

- Start a niche club. Consider cool stuff clients would enjoy. Think about activities that you love. Start a creative brainstorming club, weekly play group, or fun family outing.
- Start a product review club. People love sampling products and trying out new solutions. Give clients a taste of your work and introduce them to fun product overviews that will get them connected to your services. Invite other like-minded professionals to join you if you want to add dimension to the event.

Introduce these offerings at the end of your Book Yourself Solid Dialogue. Add, "I'd like to invite you to _____" or "Why don't you join me and my clients for a fun, playful _____." Try out different venues and topics until you discover the one that works for you. Remember, the difference between the typical client-snagging mentality and the Book Yourself Solid way is that the typical client-snagging mentality plays it safe so as not to look foolish. The Book Yourself Solid way asks, "How can I be unconventional and risky so as to create interest and excitement for my services?"

You will never be at a loss for different things to try or experiences to create for your clients and potential clients. You want to invite as many people as possible to these events for three important reasons:

1. You want to leverage your time so you're connecting with as many potential clients as possible in the shortest amount of time.
2. You want to leverage the power of communities. When you bring people together, they create far more energy and excitement than you can on your own. Your guests will also see other people interested in what you have to offer, and that's the best way to build credibility.
3. You'll be viewed as a generous connector. If you're known in your marketplace as someone who brings people together, it will help you build your reputation and increase your likeability.

3.13.1 Written Exercise: Create three ways that you can instantly add value to your potential and current clients by way of an invitation.

Getting Promoted by Others

Now let's address the second approach—getting promoted by others to speak or demonstrate. I won't address the details of being a professional speaker, someone who makes a living speaking to associations and organizations, but rather how you can use public speaking to create awareness for what you have to offer and get booked solid. If you're interested in becoming a professional speaker, pick up a copy of Alan Weiss's book *Money Talks: How to Make a Million as a Speaker* or Robert Bly's *Getting Started in Speaking, Training, or Seminar Consulting.*

If you're speaking for exposure, you probably won't be paid up front for most of the speaking and demonstrating you do, except possibly an honorarium and travel costs. You're doing it for the opportunity to address potential clients and to interest them in your offerings. There's an assumed trade involved. You receive marketing opportunities, and the association or organization that brings you in to speak or demonstrate gets great content that serves their constituents. The key is to balance the two. If you are invited to speak and you spend 90 percent of your time talking about what you have to offer, you won't be well received and you certainly won't be invited back. However, if you don't make any offers at all, you'll be sure to miss great opportunities for booking yourself solid.

Booking Your Way Up

If you would like to be promoted by others, you need to develop trusting relationships with decision makers at associations and organizations that serve your target market. In the business world, these people are often called meeting planners. At your local associations these people may be called communication or education directors or something different altogether. Bottom line: They are the people who can get you in front of your target audience.

There are thousands of associations and organizations that serve your target market. For example, colleges and universities all across the country sponsor executive extension courses, community learning programs, and all kinds of management and small business seminars and workshops. And in order to create comprehensive programs, the colleges and universities will often invite guest experts, like you, to present on their area of expertise. Trade associations and networking groups all need speakers to address their memberships, and this phenomenon has spread into the public sector as well with organizations like The Learning Annex, The Learning Connection, Shared Vision Network, and others, becoming a big part of the local communities they serve. The most potentially rewarding venues will offer:

- Large audiences.
- Audiences that include potential buyers for your products and services.
- Name recognition that is prestigious.
- The opportunity to sell products at the event (books and CDs for example).

There is a hierarchy of associations and organizations that can sponsor you and your services. I start the list with the lower-level organizations and associations and work up to the highest-level organizations and associations. Don't let the hierarchy fool you, however. You can fill your practice by speaking in front of members of the lowest-level associations and organizations, and you don't necessarily have to start with the lowest and work your way up. It may help to have previous speaking experience with some of the lower-level associations and organizations in order to get booked with the higher-level associations and organizations.

Level One

Your entry point to speaking and demonstrating is with local not-for-profit community groups or organizations like the Jewish Community Center, churches, YMCA and YMHA, service clubs, or political action groups and chambers of commerce. Some of these groups serve a particular target market, but most are made up of individuals who share similar interests. They're good places to find potential clients and even better places to work on your material and practice speaking and demonstrating in front of other people.

3.13.2 Written Exercise: Identify several level-one groups or organizations that you can contact.

Level Two

Seek out local for-profit business groups, learning programs, and schools, including schools of continuing education and networking groups like The Learning Annex, Shared Vision Network, Business Network International, colleges, and others.

These organizations are higher up the value scale for you because they serve more targeted groups of people who are really there to learn what you have to offer. Furthermore, they tend to be more prestigious than the local not-for-profit community groups.

3.13.3 Written Exercise: Identify several level-two groups or organizations that you can contact.

Level Three

At level three you'll be speaking at local and regional trade associations. There are more local and regional trade associations than you could possibly imagine or ever speak for. Do a quick search on Google.com to find associations for home-based businesses, electricians, computer programmers, lawyers, even family winemakers. Local and regional trade associations and organizations are excellent opportunities for you to connect with your target market because you know the exact makeup of your audience.

Another avenue to consider, depending on your target market and the kind of services you provide, is businesses, both large and small. I put the smaller businesses on level three and the larger corporations on level four. Many companies offer educational workshops, programs, and conferences just for their employees. Sometimes they'll bring in a speaker for a lunchtime session. Other times, the setup is more formal, and you'll speak to large groups of people at a conference center. Just be clear on why you're targeting a particular business. Know what you have to offer them that will serve their needs and what opportunities the business or the individuals who make up the business offer you.

3.13.4 Written Exercise: Identify several level-three local or regional trade associations or businesses that you can contact.

Level Four

From here you're just going to keep moving up the trade association ladder, from local and regional trade associations to national trade associations and then to international trade associations. There's even a Federation of International Trade Associations (FITA).

3.13.5 Written Exercise: Identify several level-four national or international trade associations that you can contact.

How to Find Your Audiences

Most of the information you'll need about associations and organizations that serve your target market is on the Internet. It can sometimes be difficult to identify whom to contact from a web site, but it's the best and cheapest way to start. If you're serious about using the Book Yourself Solid Speaking and Demonstrating Strategy as your go-to marketing strategy, pick up a copy of the *NTPA: National Trade and Professional Associations of the United States*. It contains the name of every trade association, its president, budget, convention sites, conference themes, membership, and other pertinent information. You might also consider referencing the *Directory of Association Meeting Planners and Conference/Convention Directors* and the *Encyclopedia of Associations* at your local library.

3.13.6 Written Exercise: Identify the decision makers for the organizations you chose in the previous written exercises. Go through your network to see whom you know who might be able to connect you with these decision makers or someone else who might know these decision makers.

3.13.7 Booked Solid Action Step: After reading this chapter, contact these decision makers using your newfound direct outreach strategies and begin getting booked to speak.

Get Booked to Speak

Meeting planners and their respective counterparts get lots of offers from people like you to speak to their constituents. That's why it's critical that you follow the Book Yourself Solid system. If you have a strong foundation and a trust and credibility strategy in place for your business so you understand why people buy what you're selling, know how to talk about what you do, have identified how you want to be known in your market, know how to have a sales conversation, are a likeable expert within your field, and have created brand-building self-expression products, not only will you get all the clients you want but you'll also earn the respect of the decision makers at the associations and organizations for whom you'd like to speak.

Do your homework. If you're going to contact a meeting planner or education director, make sure you know as much as you possibly can about their organization. You'd be surprised at how many people overlook this step and cold-call these meeting planners without having done their homework. The meeting planner knows it within minutes of the conversation.

Talk to organization members first, if possible. Learn about their urgent needs and compelling desires. They know best what they need, so learn it from them and then reach out to the decision makers. You'll get booked a lot faster that way. Even better, have a member or board member refer you. How much do we love it when other people talk about us so we don't have to?!

Send a letter or appropriate materials first and follow up with a call. And as always, be friendly, be relevant (meaning that you offer your services only if you can really serve the group), have empathy (step into the shoes of the meeting planner), and be real (no big sales pitch).

What You Need to Present to Get Booked

Each meeting planner, depending on the organization and type of event they're planning, will ask you to submit different materials in order to be considered. If you're trying to get booked at the local community center, a simple phone conversation may do the trick. If you're trying to get booked to speak at the largest conference in your industry, more is expected. You may be asked for a video, session description, learning objectives, speaking experience, letters of recommendation, general biography, introduction biography, and more. Even if five organizations ask for the same materials, it's likely each one will ask for them in their own special way. Here's a word to the wise: Make sure you follow instructions implicitly.

From time to time you will be asked to submit a video or DVD of a previous presentation you've given. If you don't have one, don't let that hold you back. As you start to speak, have your presentations recorded with a home video camera. When the time is right, you'll have your presentations professionally recorded, edited, and produced.

For a sample speaking video and related documents—including session descriptions, learning objectives, speaking experience, letters of recommendation, general biography, introduction biography, and more—go to www.BookYourselfSolid.com and click on Free Resources.

The Book Yourself Solid Guide to Putting Your Presentation Together

Now that you're going to be booked to speak, you need to put together a presentation that rocks the house. Keep your presentation as simple as possible. To be an effective speaker, you need to either teach your audience something that they don't know or haven't yet fully realized—but will really value learning—or give them an experience that makes them feel good. Ideally, you want to do both.

When putting your program together, start by considering your venue, the primary learning objectives, and the amount of time you have with your audience. I know how much you have to offer, and I know you want to give so much value that you knock people right out of their chairs. Believe it or not, you'll do that by delivering minimal content. It's likely that your audience is going to be rushing from somewhere else and then rushing to somewhere else after you've finished. It's important to never run overtime—unless, of course, you get a standing ovation and they scream, "Encore! Encore!" Then by all means, take a bow and carry on.

Plan Your Presentation

I once heard it said that experts don't necessarily know more than others, but their information is better organized. There may be some truth to that.

Knowing how to organize your information is the key to success when making any kind of presentation.

Define Your Message

To make your speech compelling, you must have something to say. It's rare that everybody in your audience will agree with your message or opinions. However, if you have a strong message—let's call it a *takeaway*—and you are very clear in the delivery of your message, even people who don't agree will listen with interest. Your entire presentation should focus on delivering the takeaway message in a clear and convincing way.

Know Your Audience

Start by considering your audience. Do as much research as you can on the people who will be attending your presentation so that your learning objectives can be directed right at their needs and desires. Work to understand the culture of the group you're speaking to so you can understand how to best communicate with them. Your audience will influence your choice of vocabulary (technical jargon) and may even influence how you dress. Knowing your audience well will also help you decide how much background material you need to deliver in order to effectively communicate your message.

Choose Your Role

In Chapter 7, one of the steps I suggested you take when developing the content for your information product was to choose the role you would be playing as the author of the information product. The same is true when creating the content for your presentation: Choose the role you're taking as the presenter. Choosing your role can help you shape the way that you prepare and present the content of your presentation.

Know Your Material

The best way to give the impression that you know what you're talking about is to really know what you're talking about. This means that you should understand your subject well and be able to answer related questions. On the other hand, it is impossible for anybody to know everything. If you're asked a question for which you don't know the answer, there is no shame in answering, "I don't know, but I'll find out and get back to you." Or you might ask if someone in the room knows the answer. Very often you'll find that someone will.

In preparing your presentation, take the time to survey friends, clients, and others in your network who represent the kind of people you'll be speaking to. Learn as much as you can about what others are saying about your topic and make sure that your presentation passes the *so what* test. Deliver it to a test audience and make sure they don't say, "So what?" at the end of the presentation.

Be Prepared

Of course you will find out where your presentation is to be held and what audio-visual equipment will be available to you, if any. You don't need to use slides or any other visual aid if you prefer not to. Over the years I've found that most slide presentations actually detract from your message. For a great guide to Microsoft® PowerPoint® take a look at *Beyond Bullet Points* by Cliff Atkinson. If you use any audio-visual equipment, check it thoroughly before you start. In fact, you may even consider making a checklist of all the things that you need to have prepared so you don't miss any important details.

Clarify how long you'll be speaking and what your audience will be doing before and after your presentation so you can incorporate that information into your planning. It's even a good idea to end a few minutes early. You'll find that, even when you bring down the house, your audience will appreciate a little extra free time.

Organize Your Information

Having a well-organized presentation can determine how well you're received. When considering your material, ask yourself, "What are the steps an audience member will need to take in order to understand the information I'm presenting?"

3.13.8 Written Exercise: The following six-step guide will help you organize your information so you're well prepared for any speaking or demonstrating situation.

Step One: To design your presentation, start by setting your main objective for the presentation. What would you like your audience to *take away* from the presentation? What idea, concept, or strategy do you want them to learn, understand, or benefit from?

Step Two: Prepare your opening. It should include:

- The purpose of the presentation—your objective
- The process of the presentation—what you're going to do
- The payoff of the presentation—what they're going to get
- The presenter of the presentation—a few words about why you're the one to make this presentation, including your web site and your always-have-something-to-invite-people-to offer

Step Three: Deliver the content of your presentation by expressing the key points of the presentation in the appropriate order. Keep it simple.

Step Four: Summarize your key points—what you just taught your audience or demonstrated for your audience.

Step Five: Offer Q&A—or mix it throughout, whatever is most appropriate for your situation.

Step Six: Close by thanking them and your host and remind them how they can continue to connect with you through your always-have-something-to-invite-people-to offer.

To Speak or Not to Speak, That Is the Question

It's important to be aware of what your talents are and to not use the speaking strategy if public speaking isn't one of your strengths. You've got to be clear about that, which isn't to say you can't get better at public speaking and performing—you can. I'm better at giving presentations now than I was when I started. What you learn by doing your first presentation you integrate into your second, and so on. However, I wouldn't suggest using the speaking and demonstrating strategy as one of your primary marketing strategies if you really aren't comfortable speaking in public or just don't want to.

Having said that, I'd like to make a key distinction: Even if you're feeling stagefright at the thought of speaking, that doesn't mean you don't have the ability to be a good speaker. I'm nervous before almost every single speech I make. I'd be worried if I wasn't because it's natural to feel nervous. If you're drawn to speaking and demonstrating and would like to give it a try, then by all means, go for it! Practice in front of a group of supportive friends or associates, or start by giving a teleclass, which may feel more comfortable. Then gradually work your way up as your comfort level and confidence increase.

No one likes to be told he didn't do a good job, and I'm no exception. Early in my career, in spite of receiving positive feedback about my presentation from many who attended, I was mortified, crushed, by the negative feedback from one or two. I ran into my biggest fear—that people would think I was stupid, that they wouldn't like what I had to say. That's my biggest conflicting intention about being a public speaker—that people will think I'm stupid. But I remind myself of the founding principle of the Book Yourself Solid way:

If you feel called to share a message, it's because there are people in the world who are waiting to hear it.

My job is to work hard to find the people who are waiting to hear my message and not to let the naysayers—the people who don't like what I'm doing—deter me from finding those I'm meant to serve. This is what drives me and keeps me going, and it's what prompts me to say again to you, if you feel called to speak, to share your message, there are people out there waiting to hear it.

The Book Yourself Solid Speaking and Demonstrating Strategy is a great way to get your message out to the world in a bigger way, allowing you to reach more of those you're meant to serve.

14

The Book Yourself
Solid Writing Strategy

Words are the most powerful drug used by mankind.

—Rudyard Kipling

Article writing is such an important way to build your reputation that I've enlisted my good friend and web writing maven, Rozey Gean from www.Marketing-Seek.com, to collaborate with me in writing this chapter because I have learned some great writing skills and marketing strategies from her. We're eager to share the Five-Part Book Yourself Solid Writing Strategy. You'll learn how to write effective articles and post them online, one of the most effective ways to generate traffic to your web site.

We'll also teach you how to analyze the different offline writing markets and the steps to get editors to publish your articles. Writing articles and publishing them online and offline will help you establish your reputation as an expert while generating interest in your products, programs, and services. By publishing online and offline, you will imprint your position as a category authority as widely as possible.

If you consider yourself a writer, you're going to say, "Yes, this Book Yourself Solid self-promotion strategy is for me and I'm going to jump on this right now!" If you don't picture yourself as a writer, you might be inclined to skip over this chapter, but please don't! Let me tell you a story that demonstrates how even nonwriters can learn to write effective articles:

My fourth-grade teacher said I had the worst spelling she had ever seen in her 25-year career in teaching. Many years later, when I told one of my childhood friends that I had sold a book to a big-time publisher, he questioned how I could do that without his help. He still had an impression of me as the kid who didn't even like to write five paragraphs for a high school essay. But I wound up writing a lot more than five paragraphs—and good ones, too!

The point is that I don't want you to miss out on this important self-promotion strategy simply because you think you can't write. If you can speak, you can write. Even if writing isn't one of your natural talents, it's a skill that can be learned well enough for you to master the Book Yourself Solid Writing Strategy and can be improved upon through practice.

How to Get Out of Writing

Does the thought of having to write an article still make you cringe? If so, don't worry. There are two other ways to gain the benefits that article writing provides without going anywhere near a keyboard:

1. Hire a ghostwriter.
2. Collaborate with a writer.

Ghostwriters are professional writers who will custom-write an article for you on the subject of your choice for a fee. Your name and business information appear in the byline and in the author's resource box at the end. Sure, it costs a little, but it's still a comparatively inexpensive marketing tool. And once you've got it, you can use it in many different ways:

- Distribute it to online article directories.
- Send it to related web sites and newsletters that accept submissions.

- Publish it in your own electronic newsletter (e-zine).
- Upload it to your own site and announce it to your mailing list.
- Submit it to print publications that cater to your area of expertise.

You can get a lot of mileage out of one article, especially if it's of professional quality.

Collaborating with a writer is another easy way to get the word out about your services. If you know someone who can write well, maybe someone whose articles you've read and admired, consider pitching a joint venture to this person. You provide the expertise, and she provides the writing skills to prepare an article based on your supplied information. Then both of your names and web site addresses appear together in the author's box at the end.

This sort of collaboration is a great way to solve the I-dislike-writing problem while effectively promoting two businesses at once.

The Five-Part Book Yourself Solid Writing Strategy

Article writing is an exciting self-promotion strategy, so let's get right to it!

Part 1: Deciding on the Subject

Part 2: Choosing an Ideal Topic

Part 3: Creating an Attention-Grabbing Title

Part 4: Writing Your Article

Part 5: Getting Your Article Published

Part 1: Deciding on the Subject

What is your subject? A subject is a broad category of knowledge—dancing, boating, fashion, business, society, and recreation are all subjects. It's possible you already know a great deal about the subject of your article, or maybe you're curious about a new subject and want to expand your knowledge of it. To help identify a direction for your writing, ask yourself these questions:

- What am I passionate about?
- What interests me on a personal level?
- What is the scope of my expertise?
- What life lessons have I learned?
- What is my target audience interested in learning?

Answering these questions will help you find good subjects. Of course, you should always remember the golden rule of writing: Write what you know. For example, if you feel stuck, consider choosing a subject that relates to your products, programs, and services, since this is probably what you have the most knowledge about.

Don't forget to explore your personal interests as well. Consider subjects based on hobbies, family, community involvement, or charity work. Your life experiences can provide you with endless ideas for article writing.

3.14.1 Written Exercise: List five subjects you would feel comfortable writing about based on your passions, your personal interests, your areas of expertise, the life lessons you've learned, and what your target market is interested in learning.

Once you've chosen one subject area to write about, you're ready to narrow it down to an ideal topic.

Part 2: Choosing an Ideal Topic

A topic is a specific, narrow focus within your subject area. Subjects such as dancing, boating, and fashion are too broad to write about, especially since article pieces are usually between 500 and 3,000 words. Have you ever noticed that most articles and books (other than reference materials) are focused on a narrow topic? The reason is simple—it makes the writing (and reading) more manageable.

Let's say you're writing about dancing. You might choose a topic like how modern dance evolved from folk dance, how dancing contributes to heart health, comfortable clothes to wear while dancing, or the growing interest in a certain style of dance.

The following examples demonstrate how to narrow a broad subject area to reach a focused topic:

From Broad Subjects to Focused Topics

Dancing → Dancing for Women → Fitness Dancing for Grannies

Dancing → Dancing for Men → Smooth Moves for the Dancing Don Juan

Dancing → Dancing for Couples → Ballroom Dancing for Latin Lovers

Boating → Water Sports → Water Skiing Safety Tips

Boating → Angler Fishing → Hot Bait for the Angler Catching Weakfish

Boating → Safety → Preventing Hypothermia

Fashion → Style → Walking in Style and Comfortable Fashion

Fashion → Seasonal Trends → Top 10 Looks for Fall Fashion

Fashion → Teens → Prom Night: Get the Red Carpet Look for Less

---

3.14.2 Written Exercise: List five focused topics you would feel comfortable writing about based on the subjects you chose in Written Exercise 3.14.1.

Determine Your Objective for Writing   Now that you've chosen a focused topic for your article, you need to establish a clear purpose or objective. Are you writing to inform, persuade, explore new territory, or to express your personal opinion? Knowing your objective will help you zero in on the content of your article. Ask yourself these questions:

- What do I want to teach the reader?
- What life experience do I want to share?
- Do I want to venture into new territory?
- How do I want to be known?

Let's examine these questions in more detail. One of the most popular types of article is the "how-to" article, where you teach your readers something. This is a great place to start, especially for new writers, because you can simply tap into an area of expertise you already have, cutting out the need for hours of research. Likewise, sharing an experience that taught you a life lesson is another straightforward way of telling a story that can really affect people.

Or you can do the research on a brand new topic, educating yourself and your readers at the same time. This keeps the writing process fresh and interesting for you.

Articles that encourage readers to take an action, such as clicking on a link for further information, are also very popular with publishers. Providing links within your item to good resources (perhaps pages of your own web site) is a great way to help your readers while establishing yourself as a reliable source of information.

Deciding now what sort of expert you want to be known as will help you determine the objective of your articles. Let's say you have a home-based accounting business. Writing a series of articles on tax tips for people who work at home is a great way to tap into your existing knowledge base while establishing a reputation for yourself as an accountant who understands the tax challenges of home-based workers. And that kind of credibility can drive new business to your door without spending a cent on advertising.

Understand Your Target Audience   So far you have narrowed your subject to a focused topic and established your purpose for writing the article. Now it is time to consider your reader.

As we discussed in Chapter 2, your target market is a group of clients or prospects with a common interest or need that you can meet. The same is true for the target audience of your article—a group of people united in their common need for the information you have to share.

To zero in on who they are, ask yourself these questions:

- What do I know about my audience—income, age, gender?
- How educated is my audience—specialized, literate, minimal education?
- How much do they already know about my topic?
- What do they need to know that I can teach?
- Are there any misconceptions about my topic that I can clear up for them?
- What is my relationship with my target audience?
- How else can I help my readers?

Digging deep to ponder and answer these questions about your readers will help you develop a mental picture of their lives and their needs. Let's say you decided to run in a marathon, but you've never run in one before. You know there must be thousands of other people out there just like you who would like to run, get fit in the process, and just feel the satisfaction of knowing they can do it. Your target audience in this case would be people who are highly motivated, health conscious, open to challenges, curious, and willing to try something new. Defining them was easy because they are just like you.

If you know that people are out there who need simple information on the topic you want to write about, and you can describe them as we just did, that knowledge will help you to define:

- *What* you will tell them.
- *How* you will tell them: your tone, vocabulary, and style of writing.

Hot Buttons   Another way to understand more about your readers is to study the emotional hot buttons that make all of us tick. Knowing what these buttons are can help you choose topics and write articles to tap into your audience's basic interests in life. You can visit this web link to get your copy of Rozey's Hot Buttons List so you can use it to inspire your next writing session: http://bys.marketing-seek.com/hotbuttons.php.

Now that you have a topic for your article, it's time to start writing.

Part 3: Creating an Attention-Grabbing Title

In Chapter 7 we talked about how the title of your information product can make a big difference in whether it sells. The same concept is true when creating attention-grabbing article titles. In fact, some writers say it's the most important part because without an arresting title, no one will bother to read the rest of your article. Here are some additional tips to help spark your creativity when writing attention-grabbing titles:

1. Select a few choice words that sum up the main point of the article.
    Example: *How to Renovate Your Kitchen Without Spending a Fortune*

2. Tell the reader what he will learn. Use specifics: "95 percent of all" or "two out of three."
    Example: *New Report Shows 54 Percent of School-Age Children Are Couch Potatoes*

3. Hint at the solution your article provides.
    Example: *Cook Low Carb Meals That Don't Leave You Craving*

4   Use questions in the title to involve the reader.
    Example: *Are You Sleep Deprived and Don't Even Know It?*

5. Curiosity is a powerful tool, so consider a teaser title.
    Example: *What Your Face Shape and Your Choice of Dog Have in Common*

6. Promise results. Explain how your article will solve a problem for the reader.
    Example: *Get Over Your Fear of Flying in Five Minutes.*

7. Promise to teach them something using phrases like "How To" or "Five Steps To Improve."
    Example: *How to Belly Dance in Three Easy Steps*

Optimize Your Title   If you're writing an article on, say, belly dancing, then you want people who are looking for this type of information on a search engine to be able to find your article. So you would do keyword research first to determine the most likely phrases your readers would use—for example, how to belly dance, belly dancing fitness, belly dancing—and then include one or two of those terms in your article title. If you determined that the keyword term *belly dancing* is searched on more frequently than *how to belly dance*, you might write a title like this: "Belly Dancing for Beginners." Or you might even incorporate two popular search terms into one heading: "Belly Dancing: Fitness Fun for the Healthy-Minded."

Search engines place a lot of emphasis on words they find in headings, so including your keywords here is vitally important to getting your article found on the Web.

Best Title Prompts   The above samples were just to whet your appetite. If you're interested in additional title-writing inspiration, guaranteed to get your creative juices flowing, visit this link for a list of 106 of the best, most attention-grabbing title prompts:http://bys.marketing-seek.com/106titles.php.

3.14.3 Written Exercise: Create five titles based on your topic choices. Remember, titles need to summarize in a few words what your article is about and be intriguing enough to make people who are interested in that topic—and even those who aren't!—want to read more. If you can fit in your top keyword phrase, so much the better!

Part 4: Writing Your Article

The Introduction   The introduction contains the nugget of your story, a short capsule that summarizes what's coming in the body of the article. It builds on the topic already presented in the title and explains why that information matters to the reader, which is why it's so important to know who your target audience is.

Some writers tend to back into their story by dropping their lead nugget down to the third or fourth paragraph, but this is a dangerous tactic. In nearly all cases, the first paragraph of your article should reflect the title, elaborate on it, and hint at all the juicy information to come.

Your introduction is also the place where you set the tone for the entire article, so be sure to speak directly to your readers using the words they use frequently. A casual style will endear you to your readers much more than an academic or technical style of writing. Above all, a strong introduction presents ideas that entice the reader to keep reading.

A compelling introductory paragraph answers everyone's most pertinent question: What's in it for me? Know how your information will benefit your readers and express that in your opening statement to them. If you can't imagine what benefit they will gain from your article, it may be wise to go back and refine your topic.

> **3.14.4 Written Exercise:** Write your lead-in paragraph by presenting the most important information first. Remember to address the topic presented in your title and explain to your readers what they will gain from your article. Here's where you get to appeal personally to the readers by telling them how you can help them learn something new, solve a problem, or simply entertain them for a short while.

The Body   The body of your article is where you fulfill the promise made in your title and lead-in paragraph by expanding on your theme. Here are a few tips to make the writing of this, the longest part of your article, easier:

- *Try to stick to one idea in each sentence and two or three sentences in each paragraph.* Concise bits of information are much easier for your readers to handle and are much less intimidating than long blocks of writing.
- *Use subheadings.* These are like mini-titles that explain what's coming next and help break up the writing into manageable sections.

Subheadings also help you organize the presentation of your information, somewhat like an outline. Put them in bold text or all capitals to make them stand out.

- *Use lists.* Giving your readers information formatted with bulleted lists, numbered lists, or any other visual device also makes the writing easier to read. The bottom line is that even the people who are very interested in your topic are in a hurry and want to get the goods fast.

- *Be consistent with your layout.* If the first item on your list of bullet points starts with a verb, make sure the first word of every item starts the same way. For example, in this list of five points, each opening sentence—the one in italics—starts with the imperative form of a verb: try, use, be, optimize.

- *Optimize your body copy.* The keyword phrases you selected for your title must also appear throughout the body of your article if you want searchers to have a better chance of finding it. Repeating these phrases just often enough to be effective without going overboard is an art form, so aim for a level of keyword frequency that reads naturally.

Going to the trouble of optimizing your article's body is worth the effort for two reasons:

1. It helps your article get listed higher in the search engine results than other content, especially if other writers don't include relevant keyword phrases in their articles.
2. It will satisfy people doing the search because you've helped them find information that speaks directly to their needs. And people (you) who help other people (your readers) get what they need are often thought of very highly and remembered!

So you can see that adding relevant keyword phrases to the title and body of your article helps both you and your readers.

> **3.14.5 Written Exercise:** It is time to write the body of your article. You need to elaborate on and fulfill the promise made in your introduction by backing up your statements with facts. Refer back to the points listed earlier if you get stuck. And remember that you don't have to get all the words perfect in the first draft. Much of writing is about rewriting and editing. At this point, concentrate on the broad strokes and allow yourself to enjoy the process.

The Conclusion   Have you said everything you wanted to say? Then it's time to wrap it all up. The conclusion is easy because it's simply a summing up of everything you just wrote. The point is to leave your readers with an easy-to-remember summary of your main theme so it is reinforced in their minds.

If you were simply to finish your article on point #9 of a list of tips, your readers would feel they were left hanging. It's human nature to crave a satisfying ending to a story. You can leave them on an even sweeter note if you share with them how they can best use the information to their advantage, and you can offer a few words of encouragement.

Write a conclusion using these guidelines:

- Restate your main points, wrapping them up in a neat summary.
- Encourage readers to try your advice.
- End on a positive note.

> **3.14.6. Written Exercise:** End your article with a strong closing. Write a conclusion by summarizing your key points from the body of the article and tell the readers how they can best use the information you just gave them.

The Author's Resource Box   This is where you get to take a bow, share something pertinent about yourself or your business, and invite your readers to take an action. It's also an important opportunity to offer your services.

At the end of every article is a separate paragraph of about five or six lines (this depends on the guidelines of each publication, so check with them before submitting). This resource box or author's bio can be used in several ways. Most authors put the following information in their resource boxes:

- A brief explanation of who they are and their expertise.
- A line or two about their business or the special offer they want to promote.
- A call to action that prompts readers to either phone, click a link, or make contact in some other way.
- *Optional:* The offer of a free gift or incentive to motivate action.

The Key to Writing Your Resource Box   To make sure your resource box is effective, clearly invite action and explain why this action would benefit your readers. This applies to whether it's signing up for a free report, a complimentary consultation, a newsletter subscription, or simply a visit to your web site to learn more about your products, services, and programs or to read more of your scintillating articles!

3.14.7. Written Exercise: Create your author resource box. Remember to include your area of expertise, your business/offer, a specific call to action, and pertinent contact information and links.

Let It Simmer and Proofread   Now take that article you have so carefully and lovingly created—and ignore it. Set it aside for *at least* a day. Return to it later and take the time to read it out loud. This is where any dropped words or weird phrasing will become apparent. Check your grammar and spelling. Polish your work to perfection. Ten rereads are not excessive; each time you'll see something that could be said better, tighter, more accurately.

A word about spell checkers: Your word processing program likely has a spelling and grammar checking function. Use it but don't depend on it. You could use a spell checker and still make spelling errors. For example, you might have typed *here* when you meant to type *hear*. The English language is complicated, and a spell checker can't comprehend which word you meant to use or should have spelled differently based on how you used it. Also share your articles with others and accept their help to spot any spelling or grammar problems that you may have overlooked.

3.14.8. Booked Solid Action Step: Compile all the accumulated elements of your research and writing to complete one article of 500 to 750 words on the topic of your choice, including the resource box. When it's polished to your satisfaction, share it with friends, colleagues, or a writing group to gain valuable insight on your writing progress.

Part 5: Getting Your Article Published

This is where the fruits of your writing labor pay off. After you have completed writing your article, you'll want to search for the niche web sites and the publications that will help share your writing with the world.

Getting Published on the Web   The Internet offers a number of unique environments to display your written work, thereby generating traffic to your web site, building your credibility, and increasing visibility for your products, programs, and services. Here are some examples:

- Article directories
- Article announcement lists
- Niche web sites
- Electronic newsletters (e-zines)

Let's take a closer look:

- *Article announcement lists.* The intent of an article announcement list is to send out e-mail announcing your article to web owners and electronic newsletter publishers who are seeking quality content.

The announcement times will vary and are set by the list owner. While many announcement lists hold your article for a period of time, they're specifically used to relay the available content at the time it gets posted—not to archive it for the search engines. See http://Groups.Yahoo.com.

- *Niche web sites.* The owner of a niche web site requires quality content written on a specific topic. The web owners' agenda is to keep their web site fresh with articles that cater to their targeted readers; they look to writers like you to supply them with this free content. See www.WebProNews.com.

- *Electronic newsletters (e-zines).* Electronic newsletters come in all shapes and sizes on varied topics. You write the content, share it with these publishers, and immediately gain access to their readers who are also your target audience. The publisher gains credible content without needing to write the articles, and you reach a larger group of prospective customers. See www.New-List.com.

For a listing of over 100 article directory submission sites and the 25 top e-zine listing sites, visit www.BookYourselfSolid.com and click on Free Resources.

Where should you start? Consider your target audience and where they're most likely to spend their time online. These are the hot spots you'll use to display your writing on a consistent basis. However, before you start the submission process, there are a few more details you need to consider:

- *Researching relevant environments.* Locate the specific environments that cater to your target audience, familiarizing yourself with the article submission guidelines.

- *Creating an article summary.* Write a short synopsis of your article.

- *Deciding on the characters per line.* Prepare different file formats for your article: Several article directories require 60 characters per line (60 cpl), while others require longer lengths. If you're unsure which format is preferred, contact the web site owner before submitting your piece.

- *Converting your article to text.* If you use a software program such as Microsoft® Word to write your article, you will be required to save it to a text file in preparation for the submission process.
- *Choosing keywords and keyword phrases.* Make a list of your keywords and keyword phrases for the article directories that require them. (These should be the same keywords and keyword phrases you used to prepare your title and article copy for the search engines.)
- *Listing the word count.* Some content sites will require a word count of your article. The total word count usually includes all words plus the title and resource box that make up your entire piece.
- *Checking your spelling and grammar.* Check your article before submission. I agree with Mark Twain, who said: "I don't give a damn for a man that can only spell a word one way." Unfortunately, not everyone agrees. One misspelled word can really turn people off.
- *Preparing an e-mail.* Write a letter to the e-zine publishers detailing what your article is about and why it would benefit the e-zine's readership. Insert a copy of your article into the body of the e-mail correspondence.

3.14.9 Written Exercise: List five article directories that serve your target market.

3.14.10 Booked Solid Action Step: Submit your article to the article directories you identified above.

3.14.11 Written Exercise: List five e-zine publications that serve your target market.

3.14.12 Booked Solid Action Step: Submit your article to the e-zine publishers you've identified above.

Consistency is the key to writing and publishing articles as a marketing tool. The idea is to saturate your target market so when a potential client is searching for valuable information, your name and articles come up again and again within the search engines' results.

Getting Published in Print   Once you're comfortable with sharing your written work online, you might consider branching out and offering articles to print publications. Writing for the print market is a highly competitive process, but it's also very rewarding.

Plan your print publishing strategy:

1. Think big but start small.
2. Request the writing guidelines.
3. Analyze the contents.
4. Write a query letter.
5. Send a self-addressed, stamped envelope (SASE).
6. Follow up with the editor.

Let's examine each step in more detail.

Think big but start small. Rather than going for the large mainstream magazines, shoot for the small focused publications such as local newspapers and magazines, trade journals, or neighborhood community newsletters. These publications are more likely to accept your work and even help edit your articles for suitability.

Once you've been accepted to write in one of the smaller publications, you can build your portfolio of printed pieces and approach the larger markets. This is important because many large-publication editors won't consider your writing ability unless they can see you have been previously published. It's similar to when you're trying to break into the speaking circuit: You start at the local level, step up to the regional level, then to the national level, and finally to the international level. It's the same concept when you're trying to get your writing in print publications.

Request the writing guidelines. Never submit articles without understanding what the publication is looking for and accepts. You need to be aware of word count, spacing format, style, and the type of information each publication is looking to include. For more detailed information on writing guidelines for thousands of print publications, pick up a copy of *Writer's Market* by Kathryn S. Brogan.

Analyze the contents. From what I hear, nothing drives editors bonkers more than receiving articles that don't fit into the theme of their publication. Your chances of getting an article accepted for print will greatly improve if you take the time to become familiar with the publication. Either purchase a subscription or several back issues; then analyze the contents by looking at items such as article length, the tone of the writing pieces, the topics covered, the balance of short articles versus long, and how many illustrations or photos were used.

Write a query letter. Now that you know which topics you want to write about and have identified the publications you want to write in, it's time to write a letter. A query letter is basically a one-page proposal that pitches your article idea. You can send a query letter about an article that has already been written or an article that hasn't yet been created, as a way to feel out the publication's enthusiasm for the concept.

Your query letter should follow the rules of a good business letter; it must immediately grab attention and convincingly (soft) sell your article idea. Use your business letterhead. If you don't own business letterhead, use white copy paper. Choose a simple font, point size 12 with single spaces. Use bullets to list key points for easier reading. Above all, be certain you spell the editor's name properly and use the correct address for the publication.

Send an SASE. Always include a self-addressed, stamped envelope along with your query letter for a reply from the editor. Have patience; it can take up to six months for an editor to reply.

Follow up with the editor. After sending your query letter and waiting the appropriate time for a response, follow up by telephone. Your objective is to inquire whether the editor is interested in your article and if she requires additional information. If the editor's response is no, don't be pushy and try to change her mind. Instead, ask her if there is a different slant to the article that might interest her or whether she knows someone else who might be interested in your piece.

3.14.13 Written Exercise: List five print publications that serve your target market.

3.14.14 Booked Solid Action Step: Submit your query letter to the print publications you identified in Written Exercise 3.14.13.

Help Editors Help You

Every publication has an insatiable hunger for good content. They're looking for articles that will inform and entertain their readers—pieces that will help them improve their lives, whether it's how to save money, lose weight, build self-esteem, or build a shelving unit.

Most editors need good writers who also happen to be experts in their field—like you. They usually have to pay top dollar to staff writers or freelancers to provide it. So if you can give them good articles at no charge, the publication saves time and money, and you get great exposure.

A solid relationship with an editor can help you gain insight to:

- What type of information is being considered for future publications.
- What kind of story may be needed in the future.
- How to strengthen your chances of being interviewed to write a particular story.

Consideration goes a long way in the print publishing business. You'll discover that the most vital component for building relationships with editors is listening and providing the best information to meet their needs. If you stay in contact with them and consistently work to supply them with good stories, you'll successfully build relationships that will provide publicity for you and your business over time.

3.14.15 Written Exercise: Decide on an ongoing schedule for submitting your articles. This can be weekly, every other week, or monthly.

3.14.16 Booked Solid Action Step: Schedule the time you'll need to write and submit new articles and then do it; or visit www.BookYourselfSolid.com and hire a virtual assistant who is experienced in online article submission and have him do it for you.

It's important to learn the art of delayed gratification. While it's natural to want instant results, this is a process, not a magic formula for overnight fame and fortune. One of the greatest mistakes I see service professionals make is giving up too quickly when their initial efforts don't produce immediate results. It's the cumulative effect that will pay off, so be consistent and be tenacious. Don't give up!

15

The Book Yourself Solid Keep-in-Touch Strategy

Be well, do good work, and keep in touch.

—Garrison Keillor

This strategy may be the most important marketing strategy you'll ever use. As you recall, you need to connect with potential clients many times before they feel comfortable hiring you or purchasing your products. If you don't have a systematized and automated keep-in-touch strategy in place, you may, as the saying goes, leave a lot of business on the table. Most important, you'll miss out on the opportunity to serve the people you're meant to serve.

The lack of a solid keep-in-touch marketing strategy is where most businesses fail. Either they bombard you with too much information and too many offers that turn you off, or you never hear from them at all, which leaves you feeling unimportant and irrelevant.

Consider the experience of my client, Barbara. Within a few short years she had compiled over 5,000 opt-in names for her database. The names were captured, but Barbara never really followed up with any of them until one day when she created a promotional offer to send to her list, and she eagerly clicked *Send*. What came back were mostly e-mails from recipients inquiring as to who she was and how they knew each other. Barbara learned a valuable lesson that day: Determine the best approach for using this strategy and build it into your keep-in-touch plans!

Each time I send out my electronic newsletter, which is my primary keep-in-touch strategy, I get new orders for my products and calls about my services. *Every time!* Without my solid keep-in-touch marketing strategy in place, I would not be able to build trust with people over time.

There is an important distinction to be made between following up with potential clients, colleagues, and others on a personal one-to-one level, and developing an automated keep-in-touch strategy where you broadcast electronic newsletters and other e-mail and send regular mail messages. When you've met someone and exchanged contact information, you have permission to communicate with him, to start or continue a dialogue that is valuable to both of you. However, this does not equate to having permission to add that person to your mailing list in order to send him your newsletter or other automated material. All of the automated follow-up that you do must be based on the principles of permission marketing, as detailed in Seth Godin's bestselling book, *Permission Marketing*. This is essential because you want to communicate only with someone who is looking forward to hearing from you. When potential customers anticipate your marketing messages, they're more open to them.

With that said, once you get to know people, you should ask them if they'd like you to subscribe them to your newsletter. Tell them about it, what's valuable about it, when it's delivered, and any other relevant information. Then, if they accept your invitation to be on your mailing list, you have permission to send it to them along with special offers and other promotions.

Relevant, Interesting, Current, and Valuable Content

It's up to you to ensure that the content you share with your potential clients through your automated keep-in-touch strategy is relevant, interesting, current, and valuable. There are six basic categories of content that meet those criteria:

1. Industry information.
2. Strategies, tips, and techniques.
3. Content from other sources (experts).
4. Product and service offerings.
5. Cool keep-in-touch.
6. Special announcements.

Industry Information

Industry information that is relevant to your target market and that may or may not be widely known is excellent content to deliver to your list. You'll position yourself as an expert within your industry while providing constant value to your current and potential clients. What's more, they will appreciate the information and your generosity for sharing it.

Let's say that you certify yoga teachers. Information regarding industry standards, regulations, and laws would be helpful to your target market. Perhaps if you were a project manager, the latest findings and announcements from OSHA would be meaningful, as would information about safety issues. Including important information in your keep-in-touch strategy also makes it more likely that your potential clients will keep the information and refer back to it, keeping you at the top of their mind for future support.

Strategies, Tips, and Techniques

This is probably the most common type of content, especially for service professionals. It's the primary type of information that I deliver to my e-zine subscribers.

Despite the appeal of this content-rich approach, many service professionals fear they will give away too much of their material. "If I

provide all these great tips and strategies for free, then why would anyone ever hire me?" they wonder. Not to worry, dear reader! Of course
there are some who will take everything you offer and never hire you or
purchase a product, but they wouldn't be hiring you anyway, and you
never know—they may be out in the world talking about what you do
and how you help. I've received tons of referrals from people who are
not clients just because I've helped them for *free*. Most people who eventually do hire you or buy your products will need to receive free advice
and support to build the trust they need in order to believe that you can
really help them. Furthermore, most people will assume that you know a
lot more than what you are giving away. They'll think, "Wow! If she
gives away this much great stuff, can you imagine what I'll get if I actually pay her?"

Content from Other Sources

I often provide my current and potential clients with relevant content
from other people so that I can over-deliver as much as possible. This gives
me a break from continuously creating content, it allows me to offer my
contacts more than I can offer by myself, and it allows me to position
other professionals who appreciate the promotion. There is an added
bonus as well: The experts I feature often return the favor by promoting
me to the people *they* serve. Isn't that a win for everybody? It's also the easiest way to create great value for the people who have given you permission to serve them when you're first starting out.

Again, if you're concerned that you'll lose customers or clients because
you highlight other experts, please recall this Book Yourself Solid principle:

> *There are certain people you're meant to serve and others you're not. If
> you can help other professionals attract business through you, you're
> creating more abundance for everyone involved.*

Product and Service Offerings

If you don't make offers to your potential clients, how will they know you can help them? If you aren't doing everything you can to serve the people who need your help, it's just short of criminal. Seriously, I believe you have an obligation to offer your services to those who need them and to those whom you know you can help in a meaningful and connected way.

Here's another way of looking at it: Most of us express our values through the things we buy. We are what we purchase. Think about it. If you didn't know me but came across my personal and business financial statements from the past three months, you'd know a heck of a lot about me, like what I value and how I spend my time. If my financial records showed that I was at the bar every night and spent most of my money playing the slot machines in Vegas, you'd get a sense of what I value. If those records showed that I attend meditation class five times a week, purchase four books a month, and spend thousands of dollars a year on private schooling for my son, you'd see a person with different values.

Most of us want the opportunity to express ourselves through the things we purchase, especially when those things are adding value to our life or work. So *please* give the people you serve the opportunity to express their values by buying what you have to offer.

With that said, making only product and service offerings to your potential clients may not be appreciated very much. Your offers must be accompanied by an over-delivery of free value. My personal goal is to subscribe to the 80/20 rule when it comes to keeping in touch. That means 80 percent of my keep-in-touch marketing is based on giving away free content, opportunities, and resources that will help the people I serve, and 20 percent is made up of offers to purchase services, products, and programs that will also help the people I serve. Remember, the people who have expressed interest in your services want to know how they can work with you, and it's your responsibility to tell them and show them their options.

Cool Keep-in-Touch

You know that I love it when you express yourself. And you also know by now that you will more easily and quickly attract your ideal clients when you do. This category is the cool keep-in-touch category because it can include any fun, different, unique, or exotic method of keeping in touch, some of which may expose your quirks! Please remember that quirky does not mean weird or bizarre. It means unusual, unique, and special. So get creative! Be bold! Dare to stand out from the crowd!

For example, Susan is a hair stylist and dog lover. Each month her keep-in-touch includes a photo shoot of her and her dogs with new fun, wild, and outrageous hair styles and colors. It is fun, memorable, and totally Susan!

What is your special, unique, and entertaining quirk that can be turned into a cool keep-in-touch strategy? The possibilities are limitless.

Special Announcements

This is a valuable method of keeping in touch if the special announcement is relevant, important, and presented as a learning tool to your target market. But be careful—it's often an overused category and can be irrelevant and annoying when it comes in the *all-about-us* form, like news about your company that is irrelevant to your contacts. How many times have you received announcements telling you about a new development in a company or about a change in management that you really cared about?

3.15.1 Written Exercise: What is the best kind of content to include in your keep-in-touch strategy based on your interests and the needs and desires of your target market?

Choosing Your Keep-in-Touch Tools

Once you've got great content to share with your clients and potential clients, you've got to choose how best to deliver that content to them. These are the most common methods:

- Electronic newsletters (e-zines)
- Printed newsletters
- Postcards and mailers
- Phone

I believe that e-zines (email newsletters) are still the easiest and most cost-effective way to keep in touch with large numbers of people. Paper newsletters can be effective marketing tools, but they can be costly to print and mail. Postcards and mailers are great for one-on-one correspondence, but again, they are costly and time-consuming endeavors when attempting to keep in touch with large groups of contacts. When you grow to a multimillion-dollar small business, we'll talk about including a paper newsletter and other mailers in your marketing campaigns to increase your touchpoints with your subscribers and contacts; but for now, let's focus on e-zines, one of the best marketing tools for:

- Building your mailing list, adding value, and marketing to your subscribers over and over again.
- Selling your products and services while you're delivering great content and adding value.
- Positioning yourself as an expert within your industry or field.
- Keeping in touch with people who've expressed interest in your products or services. You can send out one e-mail and reach all of them with the click of a button.
- Creating a viral marketing campaign (grows exponentially as it's passed along to others) because your subscribers will send it to their friends when they think it will help them.

- Creating ongoing marketing campaigns that cost virtually nothing and reap great rewards.

Ninety percent of my product and service sales are generated from 20 percent of the space in my monthly e-zine as well as through other direct e-mail promotions. Let me be clear about this because it's so important. I track my sales and know that 90 percent of my online sales are in direct response to my monthly newsletter, not from a new visitor landing on one of my web sites. As you learned in Chapter 12, your web site most effectively used is an excellent vehicle for enticing people to opt-in to your list so that you deliver value and build trust over time. Your follow-up is where you reap the financial and personal rewards of your marketing efforts.

3.15.2 Written Exercise: What kinds of tools will you use to keep in touch?

E-Zine Format

There are many ways to format an e-zine. For starters, I recommend whatever is easiest, most cost-effective, and aligned with your strengths. If you have a strong desire to learn how to edit HTML, then by all means start right now learning how to edit your own HTML e-zine. However, if you're not interested in learning this skill, farm out the work to a professional. You'll write the e-zine, send it to the professional, and she'll create the HTML version with graphics, colors, and other pizzazz.

You don't need an HTML newsletter to appear professional. Some of the most successful Internet marketers use only text e-zines. Text-only e-zines generally have a higher rate of delivery success because they tend not to get caught in spam filters. For some reason, spam filters tend to detect more HTML than plain text, and the filters block a higher percentage of HTML e-mails.

3.15.3 Written Exercise: What format will you use to send out your e-zine?

E-Zine Layout

The layout of the text in your e-zine is just as important as what you have to say. Most of your readers will not actually be reading your e-zine. First they'll scan it. Then, if the issue seems relevant and interesting, they'll read it more carefully. In order to make your e-zine compelling, easy to scan, and easy to read, follow these general guidelines when laying out your text:

- Use headlines to get your readers interested.
- Use case studies and testimonials to add credibility to your claims.
- Write from your reader's point of view.
- Write about benefits, not just features.
- Read your text out loud to make sure it sounds conversational.
- Get a colleague or customer to review your e-zine and make suggestions.
- Write as if you're speaking to one person—the person who's reading the newsletter.
- Be specific.
- Be concise.
- Keep it simple.

Make the width of your text small, especially if you're using plain text e-mail. There is an industry standard for e-mail that suggests you do a hard carriage return on your text at 65 characters or less so your text will be readable in most e-mail programs. If the text is too wide, your reader may have to scroll right and left to read it. And remember, most of your readers won't read—they'll scan. If they can't see all of the text, from left to right, they won't be able to scan.

Keep your paragraphs to no more than seven lines unless they are testimonials, and shorter paragraphs are just fine, if not better. Large blocks of text are harder to scan.

In the Free Resources section at www.BookYourselfSolid.com you can use our free tool for formatting your text e-mails. All you have to do is enter your text, click a button, and your text will be reformatted to your chosen number of characters per line—no more wasted hours editing the width of your text by hand.

Also at www.BookYourselfSolid.com are three different examples of the same e-zine: one in HTML format, one that is only text, and another that is a short text e-mail announcing that the newsletter is available online and how to get it.

Frequency

Frequency depends on a lot of factors but should be mostly based on what you're trying to accomplish with your e-zine. Some people send out weekly e-zines, some twice a month, and others monthly or quarterly. I've even seen some daily e-zines. I suggest you begin with a monthly e-zine. Weekly may be a bit much for you and your subscribers when you're starting out, quarterly probably won't get the visibility you're looking for, and daily is probably too much for most subscribers. I do a monthly e-zine plus special announcements and promotions between issues of the newsletter. That's plenty for me and for my readers.

To see firsthand how I create connection with—and value for—my newsletter subscribers, go to www.BookYourselfSolid.com and subscribe to my free e-zine now. It'll continue to help you book yourself solid.

Automating Your Keep-in-Touch Strategy

If you don't have a system for automating your keep-in-touch strategy, you don't have a keep-in-touch strategy. It's time to:

- Build and manage your database.
- Follow up with prospects and professional opportunities.

Building and Managing Your Database

I'm sure you've met hundreds, if not thousands of people over your professional life you've not kept in touch with. Now that you're a service professional wanting to attract more clients than you can handle, I'll bet you wish you had kept in touch with all those folks. Well, no matter! You will keep in touch with everyone you meet from this point forward. It is encouraging, however, to reflect on all of the people you have met with whom you did not keep in touch because it shows you how easy it can be to build a database of potential clients and networking contacts. Now that you'll put your focus on building your database, you'll be booked solid in no time.

Choosing a Database Program To have an effective keep-in-touch strategy, you'll need a reliable and comprehensive database program. There are many database programs from which you can choose, and more than I can list here, but it's important that you consider how you'll use the database program.

There are two important differentiators that I want you to consider: online and offline database building. If you're going to use the database system to collect e-mail addresses from your web site and send out e-zines and other bulk e-mails, choose a system that is designed to support this online function, like www.BookedSolidCart.com. If you're going to manage your contact information offline and do a lot of direct mail, choose a program that supports those functions, like ACT!, Goldmine®, or Microsoft® Outlook®.

I differentiate between online and offline database systems because a system like Microsoft® Outlook®, which is an offline system, will allow you to send a bulk e-mail to your entire database, but it's highly unlikely that many (or any, for that matter) of your messages will get through. E-mail servers like MSN, Yahoo, and AOL consider bulk e-mail to be spam if you're sending e-mails to over 25 or so e-mail addresses at a time without each one being delivered individually. However, dedicated online database programs are designed to overcome this problem. They send each e-mail individually so they are not considered spam.

Do some research and choose a program that best fits your needs.

Remember, the program itself is not as important as what you do with it—actually using the program to keep in touch with prospects, clients, and past clients.

Setting Up the Program   Any program you choose is going to be set up to record the basics, like name, company name, business phone, home phone, and so on. Make sure to also create categories that help you track how the person came to you (how you met or the source of that contact) and whether he or she is a client, potential client, or professional contact. This allows you to search for a group of people (such as prospects) in just a couple of seconds and send e-mails and letters to them as appropriate.

Entering Data   This is the most important aspect of the Book Yourself Solid Keep-in-Touch Strategy. Certainly you have to get a new contact's information, but that's not where most people fall short. It's that they don't actually do anything with it. You must enter and store it in the system and then continue to connect with the new contact, building trust over time. The size and quality of your database is directly proportional to the financial health of your business, but only if you use it to continue building connections with others.

Back Up Your Data   Back up your data daily. Your database is the foundation of your business. If you lose that integral support structure, you can't replace it; you're essentially starting over, which could cost you many hours of time and money.

Getting and Following Up with Prospects and Professional Opportunities

Following up with prospects and professional opportunities is a major key to your success. It's an investment that will deliver huge returns. Your Book Yourself Solid Sales Cycle is based on the success of your keep-in-touch strategy and requires you to deliver great value. Please, I implore you to make this a top priority.

3.15.4. Written Exercise: How are you going to automate your keep-in-touch strategy?

The Book Yourself Solid Keep-in-Touch Strategy is the key to ensuring that your marketing efforts are effective and successful. Keeping in touch with your potential clients is critical to developing trust and credibility, and keeping in touch will keep you foremost in the minds of your potential clients when they need you, your services, or the products and programs you offer.

Final Thoughts

This is not the end. It is not even the beginning of the end. It is, perhaps, the end of the beginning.

—Sir Winston Churchill

Congratulations! You made it through! The Book Yourself Solid system is provoking, challenging, sometimes scary, often exciting, and always powerful. The rewards you reap as a result of all your hard work will be well worth the time and effort you've devoted to this process. I hope you'll take the time now to acknowledge all that you've done because it's no small task. In fact, it's really big! We've covered a lot of ground, and you stuck with me, step-by-step, from beginning to end.

You now know who your ideal clients are and how to ensure that you're working only with those who most inspire and energize you. You've identified the target market you feel passionate about serving, as well as what their most urgent needs and compelling desires are, and what investable opportunities to offer to them. You've developed a personal brand that is memorable, has meaning for you, and is uniquely yours, and you know how to articulate whom you serve and how you serve them in a way that is intriguing rather than boring and bland.

You've begun thinking of yourself as the expert you are, and you're continuing to enhance your knowledge to better serve your market, and you understand the importance of your likeability factor. You know how to develop a complete sales cycle that will allow you to build relationships over time with those you want to serve. You've learned how to begin developing the brand-building products and programs that are a key part of that sales cycle and how to have sincere and successful sales conversations with your potential clients.

You are networking with others in a way that is genuine and comfortable, and you've learned how to build a web site that will get results, how to reach out to others in a personal and effective way, how to generate a wealth of referrals, how to use speaking and writing to reach more of your potential clients, and then how to keep in touch with the multitude of potential clients you'll connect with when implementing all of the Book Yourself Solid core self-promotion strategies.

Everything you've learned is important, but even more important is to remember the philosophy that underlies the entire Book Yourself Solid system: There are people you are *meant* to serve, and they are out there waiting for you. When you find them, remember to give so much value that you think you've given too much, and then be sure to give more.

I mentioned at the beginning of our journey that the people who don't book themselves solid either don't know what to do or do know what to do but aren't doing it. You now know exactly what to do. There are no more excuses, no more reasons to procrastinate or drag your feet or hide in your office.

The question now is what are you going to do with what you've learned? Throughout the course of this book I've given you Written Exercises and Booked Solid Action Steps that can earn you more clients than you can handle. Have you been doing them throughout the book? If you have, fantastic, keep going. If you haven't, are you going to start doing them right now? Your success hinges on your continued action.

To that end, at www.BookYourselfSolid.com we have set up a highly effective learning environment where you can continue to get support and advice about all of the concepts I've laid out in this book. If you want more support, if you want to have your own highly trained Book Yourself Solid coach, if you want to work in a structured environment that will inspire you to action and keep you accountable so that you do book yourself solid, then join one of our highly acclaimed learning programs or watch for a live event near you.

This may be the end of this book, but that doesn't have to mean the end of our work together. Your business is a generative and iterative process. You will be changing and evolving as you adapt to the ebb and flow of your growing booked-solid business, and I look forward to continuing to serve you in the best and most effective ways I can.

I sincerely thank you for spending this time with me by learning the Book Yourself Solid system. It means so much to me that you've taken the time out of your busy schedule to read my book and follow my advice. I am honored to serve you. I hope these principles, strategies, techniques, and tips make a true difference in your life and in the lives of those you serve.

Please join me on the free Think Big Revolution Monday member calls at 12:00 P.M. eastern standard time. If you do, I promise to continue to help you think bigger about who you are and what you offer the world. Join the revolution now by going to www.ThinkBigRevolution.com.

I hope the Book Yourself Solid path helps you to look in the mirror every morning and have a mad, passionate love affair with yourself, do the work that you love to do, and book yourself solid while standing in the service of others and making a difference in their lives.

I love you very much (and not in a weird way).

Think Big,

Michael Port
The guy to call when you're tired of thinking small

P.S. If there is anything that I can do to serve you, please just ask. E-mail me at questions@bookyourselfsolid.com.

References

For a complete list of all the business-building and marketing resources mentioned in this book, along with hundreds of others, please log on to www.BookYourselfSolid.com and go to the Free Resources section for immediate access.

Bayan, Richard. *Words that Sell*. Chicago: McGraw Hill Contemporary Books, 1984.

Bly, Robert. *Getting Started In Speaking, Training, or Seminar Consulting*. New York: John Wiley & Sons, 2000.

Boiler Room. New Line Cinema. Las Vegas, 2000.

Brogan, Kathryn S. *2005 Writer's Market*. Cincinnati: Writers Digest Books, 2004.

Collins, Jim. *Good to Great: Why Some Companies Make the Leap and Others Don't*. New York: Harper Collins, 2001.

Covey, Dr. Stephen. *The 7 Habits of Highly Successful People*. New York: Simon & Schuster, 1989.

Crum, Thomas F. *The Magic of Conflict: Turning Your Life of Work into a Work of Art*. New York: Touchstone, 1987.

Curtis, Dr. Glade B. and Judith Schuler. *Your Pregnancy Week by Week*. Cambridge: Perseus Book Group, First Da Capo Press, 2004.

Gerber, Michael E. *The E-Myth: Why Most Businesses Don't Work and What to Do About It*. New York: Harper Collins, 1995.

Godin, Seth. *Permission Marketing.* New York: Simon & Schuster, 1999.

———. *Free Prize Inside!: The Next Big Marketing Idea.* New York: Penguin Group, 2004.

Leonard, Thomas J. and Byron Larson. *The Portable Coach.* New York: Scribner, 1998.

Levinson, Jay Conrad and David Perry. *Guerrilla Marketing for Job Hunters.* New York: John Wiley & Sons, 2005.

Mehrabian, Dr. Albert. *Silent Messages.* Belmont: Wadsworth, 1971.

Meyerson, Mitch. *Success Secrets of the Online Marketing Superstars.* Chicago: Dearborn Trade Publishing, 2005.

Peters, Tom. *The Professional Service Firm 50 (Reinventing Work).* New York: Knopf, 1999.

Pink, Daniel. *Free Agent Nation.* New York: Warner Books, 2001.

Robbins, Anthony. *Unlimited Power.* New York: Simon & Schuster, 1997.

Sanders, Tim. *The Likeability Factor: How to Boost Your L-Factor and Achieve Your Life's Dreams.* New York: Crown Publishers, 2005.

———. *Love Is the Killer App: How to Win Business and Influence Friends.* New York: Crown Publishers, 2002.

Weiss, Alan. *Money Talks: How to Make a Million as a Speaker.* New York: McGraw-Hill, 1998.

How to Reach Us

No Matter Where You Are, Michael Port Can Help You Get Booked Solid

If you would like more information about how Michael Port or his team can help you or your organization, please visit www.BookYourselfSolid.com. There you will find information on:

- The **Book Yourself Solid™ System**, including free resources and business development products, coaching programs, and live events for the service professional
- The **Think Big Revolution™**, a free online membership club of over 5,000 big thinkers
- The **Product Factory™**, the #1 information product creation, marketing, and sales course on the Internet where you create your signature info-product in 90 days or less
- The **Traffic School™**, the ultimate Web traffic and conversion system

If you want to connect with Michael and his team today, simply fire off an e-mail to questions@bookyourselfsolid.com and someone will get back to you within the day.

Michael speaks to groups throughout the world on business development and marketing for the small business owner and professional service provider along with how to think bigger about who you are and what you offer the world. For availability please e-mail speaking@bookyourselfsolid.com.

About the Author

Michael Port and his Book Yourself Solid team have trained and inspired over 20,000 service professionals and small business owners throughout the world. He is known as "the guy to call when you're tired of thinking small" because he helps people think bigger about who they are and what they offer the world.

As a writer, he has contributed to the great work of others, including *Success Secrets of the Online Marketing Superstars* and *Guerrilla Marketing for Job Hunters*.

Born and bred in Manhattan, Michael has recently relocated to picturesque Bucks County, Pennsylvania, where, when he's not traveling, he now enjoys a quieter lifestyle with his wife Shannon and son Jake. Visit him at www.MichaelPort.com.

Index